SUFFERING AND SACRIFICE
IN THE CLINICAL ENCOUNTER

SUFFERING AND SACRIFICE IN THE CLINICAL ENCOUNTER

*Charles Ashbach, Karen Fraley,
Paul Koehler, and James Poulton*

PHOENIX
PUBLISHING HOUSE
firing the mind

First published in 2020 by
Phoenix Publishing House Ltd
62 Bucknell Road
Bicester
Oxfordshire OX26 2DS

British Library Cataloguing in Publication Data

A C.I.P. for this book is available from the British Library

ISBN-13: 978-1-912691-57-9

Typeset by vPrompt eServices Pvt Ltd, India

Printed in the United Kingdom

www.firingthemind.com

Contents

Acknowledgements

With love and gratitude to my wife Kimberly. To the memory of James Grotstein, MD, for his inspiration, and to my patients for the courage of their quest.

Charles Ashbach

It has been my good fortune to attend the International Psychotherapy Institute as a student and faculty member over many years. The value of IPI's learning community has been immeasurable and I wish to extend my heartfelt thanks to all IPI students, colleagues, supervisors, and teachers I have learned from and with.

Without the support of my family, this project would never have come to completion. My deepest gratitude goes to my husband, Jake, and my children Odette, Effie, and Rollo for their constant support and generosity.

Special thanks go to Susan Levine for emotional support when most needed, and technical advice, and to the members of her writing group for responding enthusiastically to countless early drafts.

And most importantly, many thanks to my patients, who have taught me the most.

Karen Fraley

With love and gratitude for the steady support and encouragement of my wife, Luray Gross. And in remembrance of our colleague, Geoffrey Anderson.

Paul Koehler

My deepest gratitude goes to my wife, Donna Poulton, without whose support and encouragement I may never had written a word in my life. I am grateful also for my friends and colleagues, who have helped me to shape, over the past several years, the concepts presented in this book. I would like to especially acknowledge the members of my reading groups, who love ideas and debate with admirably enduring passion; my brother and sister, who have always been available to talk at whatever depth we chose; and the faculty, staff, and students of the International Psychotherapy Institute, located throughout the world but especially in Washington, DC and Salt Lake City, Utah, for providing us with a forum to present and discuss the primary tenets of this book. Finally, I would like to thank my patients for their bravery in showing me the far corners of the human condition.

James Poulton

About the authors

Charles Ashbach, PhD, is a clinical psychologist in private practice in the Philadelphia area. He is a founding faculty member of the International Psychotherapy Institute (IPI) and director of the IPI Philadelphia chapter: Philadelphia Psychotherapy Study Center (PPSC). He is co-author of the book *Object Relations, the Self, and the Group* and the author of numerous articles and chapters. His interests include the reworking of the concept of narcissism; the psychoanalytic study of war; and the problem of chronic resistance in treatment.

Karen Fraley, LCSW, BCD, is a licensed clinical social worker in private practice in Exton, Pennsylvania, a fellow member of the Pennsylvania Society for Clinical Social Work, and a member of the national faculty of the International Psychotherapy Institute (IPI). She is an active member of the Steering Committees for the IPI's Clinical Consultants in Psychotherapy Program and Psychoanalytic Psychotherapy Program. She is a founding member of the Philadelphia Psychotherapy Study Center and teaches seminars in object relations theory and practice.

Paul Koehler, LCSW, is a clinical social worker in private practice in Doylestown, PA. A native of Pittsburgh, Paul earned his BA from Gettysburg College and his MSW from the University of Pennsylvania. He subsequently completed certificate training programmes at the Institute for

Psychoanalytic Psychotherapies and at the Washington School of Psychiatry. He is currently a faculty member of the International Psychotherapy Institute, Washington, DC. Paul's interests include literature and mythology, writing, music, lutherie, health and fitness, and the Pittsburgh Steelers.

James Poulton, PhD, is a psychologist in private practice in Salt Lake City, Utah, an Adjunct Assistant Professor in Psychology at the University of Utah, and a member of the national faculty of the International Psychotherapy Institute (IPI). He currently serves on the Steering Committee for IPI's Psychoanalytic Psychotherapy Program, is the chair of IPI's Curriculum Committee, and is the past co-director of its Salt Lake City chapter. He has written numerous articles and chapters on psychological treatment and theory, and is the author of *Object Relations and Relationality in Couple Therapy: Exploring the Middle Ground* and co-author of *Internalization: The Origin and Construction of Internal Reality*. He has also co-authored two books on the history of art in the American West: *LeConte Stewart: Masterworks* and *Painters of Grand Teton National Park*.

Note to the reader

For purposes of confidentiality and privacy, the names and identifying details of all of the patients described in this book have been disguised.

For ease of reading, when non-specific situations are being referred to, "she" is used for the counsellor or therapist and "he" for the client or patient, but, at any point, the opposite gender can be substituted.

The infant tends to be "he" when discussed in relation to the mother to avoid confusion over to whom "she/her" is referring.

Foreword

Giuseppe Civitarese

I have always thought of theology, if seen as psychology in the form of narrative, as the most refined expression of what men know about themselves. In *Suffering and Sacrifice in the Clinical Encounter*, the authors use a figure from the Jewish and Catholic religions, Abraham, and a pivotal moment from his life: the episode of offering his son Isaac as a sacrifice to God. The central idea is to explain some of the more challenging kinds of psychological illness through the dynamics and meaning of ritual sacrifice. As Fairbairn (1943), quoted on p. 89, says, "It is better to be a sinner in a world ruled by God than to live in a world ruled by the devil."

The fact is these patients reveal themselves as devilishly difficult. Similar to the pseudo-neurotic patients described by Bion which recur massively to transformation into hallucinosis as a defence, they don't seem overtly severe; quite the opposite, they can be brilliant and well adapted. With the passing of time, however, therapy becomes a sacrificial ritual in itself. The analyst feels its lack of vitality with exasperation. The patient is always complaining about the same things. He lives but doesn't feel he lives, and torments and devalues both himself and the analyst. Resistances are tenacious and the so-called negative therapeutic reactions frequent. The analyst wonders if, perhaps, they are intractable patients.

The main difficulty to face is the deep sadomasochistic drive by which these patients seem to be dominated. It is as if they are intent, all the time, on sacrificing themselves to a cruel inner deity in the hope of reconciling with it and thus being left free to exist. Each of them has developed a kind of 'private religion'. Instead of an emotional position of openness and hospitality, this religion results in a fanatical moralism. As we know, moralism rather makes room for abstract and preconceived ideas, and therefore shows little concern for human interest. Rigid respect for the norm occurs at the expense of vitality and it leads to living as robotic beings incapable of 'feeling'.

From the point of view of psychoanalytic theory, it is important to have an idea of how this cruel superego and enemy of life could have been generated. It appears that it is formed in subjects for whom the experience of the non-breast or the absence of the breast that is at the origin of thought is not tolerable. To put it another way, the rhythm of positive and negative experiences given by the encounter of a preconception of the breast with concrete satisfaction and then by the encounter with a non-satisfaction is too much infiltrated with the negative of painful absence (Civitarese, 2016a, 2019). The object does not provide enough truth as food-for-the-mind. Things can be so irreparable that this absence (even in the shape of a 'too much' of imminence) leads to structuring a psychotic personality. Then the severity of the superego only reflects the hyperbolic degeneration of any disattunement with the object into a feeling of dread. The reason for this is that the slightest lack is resented as virtually catastrophic. As Tustin (1972) imagines for autistic children, absence is felt as the amputation of a part of the body.

When this is the imprint received from the primary relationship, the infant's instinctive reaction is to stick to the object to plug its holes. The total identification with the ruthless object, the non-distance from it, drastically reduces the degree of freedom of the subject with respect to the norm. Responses to stimuli tend to become fixed and 'automatic'. As it entails differentiation from the object, simple existence is already a fault. That's why basically a cruel superego and any form of moralism are against life. As in Kafka's *The Trial*, the dominant feeling is nameless anguish and a kind of passive resignation. Of course, attacks are not only directed at the self, in terms of the manifest symptom we define masochism, but also at the object and the analyst, and here we would use the word sadism. The paradox is that the unconscious meaning of any kind of sadomasochism is precisely, even if through hatred, to earn the love of the object. To be alive in the sense of feeling vital—according to the definition of this term, being capable to live—is felt as guilt.

In fact, we have to presume that at the centre of the self, there is a void, which very likely is what remains from a trauma suffered at a very early stage of life. The main thematic area explored by the authors is clearly that of the primitive states of mind and of how these traumatic experiences can find in analysis an opportunity for representation or figurability and transformation. Achieving this goal is not simple. Such patients assume a posture of moral authority that implies superiority, perfection, and purity, which should lead them to the Freudian triad of "joy, exultation and triumph" (p. 121), and so challenge the therapist's capacity to stay there and remain alive and receptive. The reason is that renouncing their defensive organisation would be tantamount to suffering agony. The analyst should not get involved in the same magically salvific, and therefore masochistic, self-sacrificing, climate. There are limits to the possibilities of treatment. On the other hand, the therapist should be the object that can gradually help the patient to free himself from this addiction to arrogance. In this perspective, the significance of the concept of negative capacity and faith, and the resulting technical principle of listening without memory (voluntary), without desire (zeal) and without understanding (intellectual), is emphasised.

The revisitation of the oedipal (and pre-oedipal) drama, which is what goes wrong in these patients, is extremely evocative. We read amazing sentences—about symbolic (non-pathological) patricide/matricide—such as: "This murder starts out so minutely, so benignly, and so incidentally that it is hardly noticed as such: we learn to feed ourselves and to walk without assistance; we learn how to dress ourselves and to tie our own shoes; we learn how to read and to explore the world on our own; we learn how to compete in a sport or to play an instrument. With each of these little successes, these little victories, these little murders, we sever a part of our dependence on our real or symbolic parents and we claim an increasing responsibility and an increasing authority for ourselves" (p. 64). Now the expression used, "little murders", which could be the title of a novel by Agatha Christie, makes us think. These little 'assassinations' are normally paid ("atoned") with the formation of the superego. The verb 'atone' here is noteworthy because it is linked to 'atonement' as a religious concept and to Bion's *at-one-ment*, in which it represents the central mechanism for 'making a mind'.

Naturally, the more there have been failures in the mother–child dance at birth and the more severe this superego is, the more the at-one-ment risks deteriorating and becoming an imperious need for total fusion at the expense of the possibility of growth and differentiation. Very pertinent and intriguing are also, on one side, references to the institution of the original temporality, or of the capacity "to suffer time", as the felicitous outcome of this process; and, on the other, to timelessness and other forms of disturbances of temporality as the failure of this same process. When there is a withdrawal into autistic shells, time is suspended through a dissolution (*unlink*) of the three modes of experience of past, present, and future that constitute it (or rather of the dialectical game that binds them to each other) and their collapse and agglutination in a whole as fused and still: then everything is organised around the cult of a god-object and the sense of superiority that gains from it.

But the Oedipus story is complex. Between patricide and incest lies the episode of the plague at Thebes and the confrontation with the Sphinx, followed by the latter's suicide. In his essay on arrogance, Bion (1957) proposes to see in *this* episode and not in the sexual crime the real theoretical treasure of the Oedipus myth. The sin of excess and arrogance lies—despite Tiresias' warnings—in wanting to know what *cannot* be known. The subsequent incest would be nothing more than an allegorical figure of this same sacrilegious curiosity that generates *monstra*. Like Oedipus, who sacrificed himself to save Thebes, the patient is the very prototype of the unknowing scapegoat; not only the sacrificial victim, but also the high priest of a private religion. The fact is that often this position is mirrored by the analyst who also behaves as the high priest of the positivist religion of an epistemic psychoanalysis; a psychoanalysis excessively based on intellectual understanding and not enough on becoming and being (Ogden, 2019).

So a possible subtitle I imagined for *Suffering and Sacrifice in the Clinical Encounter* could be 'Investigation of the origin of the cruel superego', an issue of the utmost interest—I dare to say—for *any* kind of psychic suffering we see in our consulting room and also as a key issue for the renovation of our theories. As in a good jazz session, the various contributions appear like happy variations on this core theme. Multiple vertices are used successfully. Concepts such as primitive agonies (Winnicott), the dead mother (Green), zones of non-existence (Bion), psychic retreats (Steiner), mutual captivity (Ogden), and the inaccessible unconscious find a new context in which their theoretical and heuristic value is demonstrated and expanded. The theory employed is rich and versatile, the clinical vignettes extremely vivid and instructive. The style of the book is happily communicative and allows a pleasant and rewarding read. *Suffering and Sacrifice in the Clinical Encounter* is a generous book, with a remarkable unity of theme and style, fruit of vast experience and love for psychoanalytic knowledge. The central image of patients who are difficult to reach as followers of a fanatical religion that forces them to continuously sacrifice the scapegoat—depending on the case, alternatively or simultaneously—of either aspects of self or of the analyst to a tyrannical god, is memorable. As a powerful metaphor it can help theoretical understanding and guide clinical work. I can only recommend reading this fascinating and brilliant book to all analysts, psychotherapists, and scholars of human sciences interested in using psychoanalysis to understand humanity and alleviate psychic suffering.

Introduction

Charles Ashbach, Karen Fraley, Paul Koehler, and James Poulton

There is a type of patient encountered in the practice of dynamic psychoanalytic psychotherapy or psychoanalysis that presents as very motivated, with average or better intelligence, and with apparent life success, sometimes impressively so, but also with a deeply dissatisfied experience of his own character and accomplishments or, one might say, of his very essence. The treatment, which seems to start so well, after some time—months or even years—feels to have descended into a kind of agonising and repetitive stuck process that fails to achieve a deeper level of insight, understanding, and relief. Before too long we come to feel afflicted, even tormented by the patient's repetitive complaints and by the rote recitation of a narrow and shallow range of memories and associations along with the litany of continuing complaints concerning the failure to achieve greater satisfaction in his work, relationships, or love life.

The patient insists on maintaining the frame and continues to come to sessions even though no further progress seems possible. From the therapist's point of view the treatment seems to have devolved into an agonising, stuck process resembling an empty and tormenting ritual. A desperate frustration often emerges in the therapist, along with strong feelings of guilt, shame, and impotence. A cloud of inadequacy penetrates the field between patient and therapist, raining down doubt and confusion about the viability of the therapeutic process—is the therapeutic baby alive and breathing, or is failure, or death represented in the therapeutic impasse?

Gregorio Kohon (1999), in his cogent and useful paper "Dreams, acting out, and symbolic impoverishment", describes how this category of patient often suffers from having "turned away from the primary object both prematurely and in hatred" (p. 80). It is both the prematurity and the hatefulness characteristic of this turning away—in reaction to early childhood trauma—that creates enormous turmoil and dissatisfaction for these patients in their lives and for us in our efforts to engage them therapeutically.

We have found that this traumatic turning away from the primary object was not necessarily prompted by obviously or dramatically traumatic events but often seems to have been prompted by a less obvious, but no less traumatic, lifeless indifference—by the absence of delight, joy, and vitality—in the mother's early nurturing characteristic of the "dead mother" (Green, 1986). Unable or unwilling to remember or represent those experiences, these patients can only convey them to us by way of their subtle or not-so-subtle expressions of "No", through inscriptions or behaviours in the transference relationship.

Thwarted in our attempts to make or sustain emotional contact, our increasing anger—our counter-"No"—sometimes moves us to make harsh or sadistic interpretations or judgements, all the while feeling helpless, sometimes desperately so, in the face of our patient's hateful refusal to allow ordinary therapeutic contact. Our potentially helpful and liberating recognition of the limits of our therapeutic capacities and of the potential hazards of our therapeutic ambitions may then deteriorate into a hostile or indifferent retreat that tragically replicates the scornful despair and hopelessness this patient has lived with since childhood.

This book seeks to offer the reader a particular paradigm through which this type of patient can be appreciated in a dynamic and alive way, utilising the multiple perspectives of a wide range of psychoanalytic theories and guidelines for practice. We seek to illuminate and elaborate what became known as an intense and chronic resistance that Freud (1923b) identified as the impenetrable circumstance of the patient's "negative therapeutic reaction" (p. 49) and offer a reframing of the concept to reveal the underlying traumatic crisis of radical alienation that the subject suffers from behind the boundary of his so-called "resistance".

Our work together as senior faculty at the International Psychotherapy Institute inspired us to study the particular violence we sensed behind the intense resistances found in these patients. As we listened to our students and our supervisees we noticed a pattern of increasing frustration, dismay, and shame accompanying their work with these patients and a palpable tendency to invest more—more energy, more supervision, more effort—into the challenge of dealing with the patient's "intractable" problem.

Concurrently, in the aftermath of the September 11 terrorist attacks, we turned to Franco Fornari's classic book, *The Psychoanalysis of War* (1975), for guidance and understanding as we tried to fathom those catastrophic social events. He saw in the collective the emergence of intense feelings of guilt and responsibility when the primary love object was experienced as damaged or lost. The war impulse arose to cover over the group's phantasy (this spelling used to specify the unconscious nature of the experience) that their imagined sadistic attack against the love object was at the core of the catastrophe. In such a context an external object is used as a scapegoat surrogate (Girard, 1977) to stand in place of the self, individual or collective, to absorb all guilt and blame for the evil power of the external Other. The experience of mourning is stopped and instead transformed from the sorrow, guilt, and remorse for the loss or damage of the love object into the "killing" of an enemy assumed to be the "destroyer" of the love object. Fornari (1975) stresses this attack against the object is a "security organisation" (p. xvi) that operates as a defence against the subject's "*psychotic anxieties*" (p. ix, our emphasis). In the clinical situation, then, the patient's impenetrable resistance reflects a similar condition of existential dread associated with his ultimate "crime" (killing the figure of love and dependence) and the attempt to extrude the crime into the person of the external bad object. This is the essence of the "paranoid elaboration of mourning ..." (ibid., p. xviii).

We also found the anthropological insights of Girard (1977) and the cultural insights of Bergmann (1992) to be important guideposts for understanding the mythic foundation of primitive mental states. Their studies of primitive cultures showed in a way similar to Fornari how human beings, in a context of loss and crisis, regress to a primeval psychic–emotional position that views the violent destruction of precious resources, especially human sacrifice to be the necessary means for propitiating and atoning to a deity, that is, a supernatural figure of ultimate power and moral authority, for their failures, sins, and crimes. We understood how this attitude of guilt and primitive atonement came to constitute the unconscious, sadomasochistic attitude of the aggressively resistant patient and thus became central for understanding the unique and paradoxical transference and countertransference responses that characterise the treatment of this individual.

As we elaborated and knitted together these various vertices of understanding, we were able to conceive and imagine a process of psychic implosion and collapse following the experience of early traumatic events which diminished or precluded the child's (patient's) capacity to experience and internalise a solid and reliably loving attachment experience with the primary object, be it mother or father. This primal "lack" (Lacan, 1977, p. 259)—which is at once an absence and an injury—led to the collapse of a durable psychic structure and further to the construction of a substitute, compensatory system of internal objects. Denied the experience of real contact with sustaining objects the subject creates, manically, out of his omnipotent phantasies and desires an ideal object of an imagined perfect maternal figure as well as an all-bad object that acts as the container for the hatred and vengeance directed against the abandoning figure of the lost mother.

Following Freud's (1907b) observation, we began to see how these patients' regression to the depth of their personality sought to transform the therapeutic relationship into a "private religion" (p. 119) organised around the "rituals" and ceremonies of suffering and sacrifice, and came to appreciate the inadequacy of the term resistance to accurately describe the crisis of psychic deprivation and catastrophe that marked the core of this type of patient's inner world. This patient, following the judgement of his primitive superego, believes with a religious conviction that he is completely and utterly responsible for the damage done to the good object and a compensating sacrificial process must be continually engaged to deny and negate his feelings of complete guilt for the catastrophe. Thus, resistance could now be understood as a boundary condition that marks the point of the crisis of the self which is hidden behind the false-self (Winnicott, 1960) mask of the paradoxically innocent and guilty patient. The patient seeks to remain a stranger to himself in order to escape the threatening burden associated with his unconscious hatred and aggression.

Freud's (1907b) concept of the "private religion" (p. 119) and Fornari's (1975) idea of the "paranoid elaboration of mourning" (p. 103) are organised both around the breakdown in the subject's ability to differentiate between illusion and reality as well as around the perverse need for the power to destroy the categories that define reality: differences in sex and generations. The patient's experience of object loss has caused his regression to the deepest psychic layers of the mind with the activation of radical splitting leading to fragmentation and the loss of the sense of personal responsibility. The subject in search of an absolute figure of power and protection creates an ideal god-object and sets about sacrificing to it to fend off the unbearable burden of guilt and shame. The devotion of the subject provides the illusion of the goodness of the self and his protestations concerning his adoration of his deity assert his innocence and purity. Having undergone such a radical transformation he can now say:

> As can be seen through my sacrifices I am a good, loyal and humble servant and the damage to the love object is not related to my weakness or lurking hostility but to the malicious activities of the evil-Other. To demonstrate my love I will attack and punish that figure for its crimes and will take revenge upon it.

Fornari (1975) underscores the problem of suffering guilt as the key to understanding such elaborations avoiding mourning and he writes: "The need to accuse someone else of the death of a loved person is the most obvious proof of *man's incapacity to bear guilt in the occasion of mourning*" (p. 55, original emphasis).

We have found that the problem of unconscious guilt cannot be underestimated. The challenge of suffering guilt constitutes the lynchpin of psychic growth, the turning point from which a narcissistic fusion with the ideal shifts to awareness of the self as separate, limited, small, and sometimes helpless to prevent the loss of a loved one. With the type of splitting described earlier, responsibility is fragmented (Segal, 1987), resulting in lack of clear accountability and compromising the capacity to inhabit one's particular and limited life. Riviere (1936) points out that the subject is tormented by the primary necessity to maintain the wellbeing and perfection of his love object, the unconscious primary object at the core of Klein's (1935) depressive position, and where the object is damaged or lost he feels that nothing may be done for himself until the object is completely and utterly restored. A type of unconscious sacrifice takes place through the transformation of the therapy into a sacrificial ritual.

Bergmann (1992) describes two forms of sacrifice. In the first, older form, hostility and persecution are projected into the deity so that "He" is established in an especially violent and ferocious form reflecting the common experience of the superego of the group. Fear and terror of the deity's persecuting recriminations and condemnations take hold and the deity is felt to demand an exclusive and costly sacrifice to appease his anger. The sacrificing people atone their guilt through the propitiating action of the sacrifice of a valuable resource, most importantly the killing of an alive and valuable object. In response, the deity is felt to look favourably on the special ones who offered the sacrifice, softening his hostility and persecution into love and acceptance. The sacrificers are now the chosen people, secured in their connection with the deity, who is now obligated to extend a loving and protective hand in return. Examples of this type of sacrifice abound in classical myths, as we see in the sacrifice of Iphigenia by Agamemnon to appease the wrath of the goddess Artemis, who responds by turning the winds in favour of the Greek army, speeding their way to make war in Troy.

A second, more humane and communal form of sacrifice follows the group's development of a more mature superego where the deity (superego-ideal) is felt to be more benevolent and shares the sacrifice with the community. In this scenario a sacrificial beast is killed and the best parts of the meat are given to the deity, while the group consumes the rest. This is seen today in the Christian ritual of communion. Here the deity and the sacrificers share the strength and nourishment of the beast, the offering that "gives" its life for the worshippers, and bonds of love and gratitude unite both aspects of the community. This form of belief and sacrifice affirms the importance of love alongside the violence of the destruction of the offering.

The form of sacrifice used in this book is derived from the earlier, more primitive and ruthless form of the relationship between the subject and his deity. In the clinical context, the traumatically abandoned patient feels the violence of his radical separation from primary objects as a punishment and constructs his god-object in line with the violence that is at the core of his alienated circumstances. In primitive cultures a vulnerable, dependent, and vivacious object (a child or kid goat), considered to be innocent, carries the projected sins and guilt for the sacrificers (family, group) and must be destroyed, typically through burning, that is, in the Holocaustic mode. As the group believed their sacrifice atoned for the guilt of their sin and united them with their god-object, so the patient at an unconscious level expects a similar release from the agony of disconnection from his deity. The sacrifice substantiates and enriches the power of the god-object, a manic restitution of the ego-ideal and the followers, here the patient, secure the promise of deliverance from pain and suffering.

An important aspect of this primitive form of sacrifice is that emotional pain (guilt, loss, perdition) is magically dissipated rather than worked through and integrated. Emotional agony and shame are likewise dissipated rather than experienced, represented, suffered, and accepted. We use the term "*regressive* suffering" to refer to the defensive function of the enacted sacrifice that takes place through the repetitious and empty ritual of the clinical sessions that seeks to avoid the pain of accepting loss, helplessness, and the tasks of working through in the depressive position. In this version of treatment the patient feels pain in a masochistic mode, with the goal of evacuating it out of the self, that is, without seeking to transform it into understanding and growth. In such a setting the therapy partnership cannot produce the baby, the new life of the self as all forms of pleasure, sexuality, hope, and generativity are also sacrificed on the altar of guilt.

Where the patient accepts the working-through process of the treatment and identifies and carries the burden of the guilt and shame forward towards understanding and integration we consider that to be "*progressive* suffering". This process is predicated upon the establishment of a bond of safety and acceptance within the relationship by means of the mitigation of the subject's harsh superego and the recognition that the ideal replacement object must be relinquished. In such a setting the patient might be able to work towards the mourning of the loss of the primary object and the ability to derive more pleasure from the growing success of the treatment. Bion (1962) observes how such an experience enables the subject to "learn from experience" and as he can suffer pain so he is able to "suffer" pleasure (Bion, 1965). An example of the reluctance to accept emotional pain was expressed by a patient who said, "If I turn back towards all the pain inside, then I will know it really happened and I will have to accept there is nothing I could do about it."

We can see how the patient's use of regressed suffering leaves him completely in the role of the victim, where he experiences life as having descended upon him, as fate or bad luck but not related to his choices or desires. He remains chronically innocent and bears no responsibility for his experience, and accordingly is unable to understand and accept the tragic pattern of his life. In such a state the patient seeks to disable the forward movement of the treatment by reversing the roles. Now the therapist must suffer the guilt, shame, and impotence the patient feels; must apologise for the errors of her ways and must make the joylessness of the treatment her total responsibility. The patient, identified with the internal bad object of the aggressor feels relieved of the moral burden of his conscience and is able to look down on the therapist and use her as his scapegoat surrogate.

The patient, trapped within the unconscious experience of his radical ambivalence and psychic fragmentation, moves between seeking to activate his hatred and vengeance, by tormenting and frustrating the therapist or activating his desire to give and receive some measure of love and care that might lead towards separation and understanding. This double-bind condition of love and hate freezes the patient in the agony of a constantly repetitive relationship. He sacrifices the therapist as stand-in for the original lost loved object and sacrifices himself in his confusion about who is to blame for the crisis of his life and psyche. But because of psychic fragmentation, the subject can take almost any external figure or part of the self and use this object to act as the container for the patient's guilt, shame, and self-condemnation.

Because self and object are interchangeable in the unconscious, the designated sacrificial aspects of the patient's personality—that is, their vulnerability, dependency, or vivacity—may be projected on to, inscribed into, the therapist, or into any other person separate from the patient. When this occurs, the therapist or other figure becomes the sacrificial victim, in the sense that their skills are devalued, their achievements erased or negated, their liveliness deadened, or their significance as a figure of dependency denied. This recognition helps to explain why therapists working with this type of patient experience a wide range of painful and overwhelming countertransferential responses. The sacrifice of the therapist or the therapy, then, can be seen as a displaced but potentially representable form of the sacrifice of the self.

Clinical implications/considerations

The clinical situation with the chronically resistant patient presents the therapist with a series of daunting challenges. First, we have to adjust our expectations and therapeutic stance to accommodate the fact that the subject's internal world has become part "crypt" and part "fortress", reflecting the trauma of the loss of his primary figure of attachment and the collapse of his psychic structure. It is this bifurcated world that exists behind the boundary condition of the patient's resistance. Unable to function without connection to an alive and available primary, internal figure, the subject establishes an internal ideal figure (replacement object) that he possesses and controls that allows him to deny the loss of the actual object and keep alive the hope of reversing his psychic tragedy. The ideal object functions as a "fetish" figure (an object used to cover over a missing reality; Freud, 1927e) to protect against the emergence of feelings of panic, madness, and completely alienated aloneness.

Second, a damaged, reproachful internal object is internalised as the bad object (superego component) that continues to attack and judge the subject for his responsibility in causing the loss of the primary object. Here a distorted sense of "omnipotent responsibility" (Wurmser, 2013, p. 27) causes him to feel chronically guilty, morally shamed, and relentlessly haunted. To bear up under the ruthless clash of his love and hate the subject radically splits himself into a condition of a dissociated, double-psychic reality.

Third, the patient seeks to transform his intrapsychic conflicts into interpersonal, *moral* ones (Britton, 2003) so that he may externalise them and feel justified in continually attacking the therapist (as stand-in for the actual lost object) and dominate her through manic triumph, humiliation, and obsessive control. The shame that the patient was forced to endure as a child becomes a weapon in his hands to both force the therapist to suffer in his place, what we have termed the scapegoat role, and as a communication to the therapist to demonstrate the savagery of his childhood experiences. In this way the treatment becomes saturated with an accusatory and relentless tone, inscribed into the soul of the therapist that allows for no resolution or relief and leads to states of intense and miserable countertransference.

Fourth, the patient is clinically depressed and suffers anxiety, persecution, mania, and excessive grievance due to the grave distortions of his primitive psyche, where he feels absolutely guilty and must project outward the bad parts of himself. This projection leads to what Fornari (1975) describes as the "paranoid elaboration of mourning" (p. 103) and the subject will not allow the recognition of his situation in order to deny the reality of his loss and aggression. This stance enables the patient to be free of any sense of gratitude for the therapist's help and support or any feeling of responsibility for the guilt he experiences for his incessant, sadistic attacks against the therapist.

The affect states become intense and tormenting, reflecting the double bind of wishing for relief and chronically preparing for battle. Rosenfeld (1975) speaks of the subject's "omnipotent inner structure" (p. 221) as being loaded with envy that attacks both the dependent part of the self and the needy part of therapist. In this way we can understand that the subject's exclusion from the emotional and narcissistic centre of the mother's world has left him destitute and deprived of the investiture of the mother's acceptance and joy of life. As Bion (1962) observes, such individuals have not been able to satisfy their need for love, understanding, and mental development and therefore deflect such needs into a search for "material comforts" and the need for love turns into "overweening and misdirected greed". The patient is often the individual that "appears to be incapable of gratitude or concern either for himself or others" (Bion, 1962, p. 11).

The sacrificial act we describe in this book is an unconscious enactment of a primal phantasy (Wurmser, 2007, p. 268) where the subject's destruction of a therapeutic good, on the altar of his "private religion" (Freud, 1907b, p. 119), constitutes a sacred offering to his deity, the subject's self-created ideal god-object. The primary benefit of the sacrifice in the patient's desperate belief is the magical inversion of his catastrophic loss transformed into the deity's gratifying answer of fulfilment and union: the original object reappears and the unbearable gap between self and the maternal object is closed. There is no observable event in the session, only the patient's behaviour or communication indicating his refusal to accept the offering of the therapist. The sacrificial act both affirms the subject's complete loyalty to his god-figure, repudiating the therapist, and at the same time is a vengeful act against the therapist, now felt to be the original tormenting, parental object. Vengeance and sacred loyalty are combined in this one paradoxical moment.

In a way this act is a "human sacrifice" (Grotstein, 2000, p. 221) because the depth of the therapist's being is offered to the patient by means of her understanding and interpretations and the rejection of her care and understanding triggers a great loss and narcissistic insult as well as an outbreak of anxieties, seeming to confirm for the therapist that she is the reason for the patient's suffering and misery. The subject at the deepest level of his personality can feel annihilated by the perverse circumstances of his childhood and therefore it is perhaps not too dramatic to consider the patient's renunciation of the therapist's contributions a brutal act of cruelty and indifference (psychic murder?) that the patient has felt so many times throughout his development. It is the continual frustration of the therapist's offerings, ideas, and associations that lead to the buildup of a very pernicious and toxic form of the counter-transference that undermines the therapist's capacity to remain symbolic and not to react from the damaged parts of her personality.

The treatment process with a traumatised patient involves a long-term experience of the interpenetration of the therapist's self by the patient. The patient suffered the collapse of psychic structure and with that the weakening of his ego as well as the intensification of his superego in a primitive and attacking mode. Having suffered the loss of the primary figure, the subject has a chasmic void in his psyche that he seeks to fill with the ideal figure of the god-object. He continues to experience the paradox of his schizoid retreat against the therapy or, in a full-fledged assault, to merge or fuse with the therapist. Both conditions can threaten to overwhelm the therapist's position of manageable balance and containment felt in the countertransference. The therapist must work to first survive the chaotic and at times psychotic elements in the transference and, having mastered that, must seek to recover her mind and feelings so that she can begin to function once again as a symbolic, thoughtful, and sensitive container for the storms continuing to emerge from the patient.

Racker (1968) warns therapists against the dangers of *masochism* hiding in our empathy and of *sadism* hiding in our ambition. We seek the patient's affirmation in order to feel that our therapeutic care is actually real and effective and, what's more, that it is appreciated. The patient has an awareness of our motivations and can tell whether or not we understand and can appreciate the existential dimension of the crisis of his circum-stance. The movement out of the register of the narcissistic, the perfect, and ideal requires an enormous amount of courage, faith, and hope, and the patient must gain some recognition that we appreciate the scope of his efforts. Such movement means that he is trying to descend down out of the mythical–magical narcissistic register of his injured unconscious into the register of reality-testing in the context of object relations, where progress is achieved through the hard work of reflection and integration and not through the power of moral purity and wish. We might even consider that the patient must forgo the pleasures of his imagined perfect feast in order to be able to participate at the table of the therapy meal prepared by the clinical partnership.

The class of patient we are addressing includes those that suffer from primitive mental states. Victims of trauma erect barriers against the re-experience of the original catastrophic circumstances and can manifest the most intransigent resistant positions against the re-emergence of perverse and primitive experience and psychotic states. Likewise, the subject's identification with the aggressor objects leads to a perverse attitude towards the differences between the sexes and the generations. The sexual impulse loses its value in the generating of a new "life" in the treatment, the new child emerging from within the patient, and becomes degraded as a seduction or hysterical means of control, distraction, and complicity. Lurking behind the sterile sexuality of the traumatised patient is the wish not for new life but the attempt to "open the door to the past" in order to find an infantile retreat from the dangers of growth and maturity.

Lombardi's work (2016, 2017) seeks to support the patient in establishing a deeper and more compelling integration of the split, fragmented, and dissociated emotional network of feelings and experiences that protect the subject from reactivating the original trauma within his body. Our careful, slow, and sensitive containment efforts assist the subject in organising a "vertical connection" within his body so that the essential "body–mind link" (2017, p. 94) can be made (an internal vertical experience) and blocked feelings and memories can be accessed and liberated or, where they were unrepresented, they might be assembled from the material of the present. As the subject begins to come alive, the "horizontal relationship" (Lombardi, 2017, p. 94) between us can be strengthened with the subject neutralising some of the primitive horror and dread of his earliest experience. We move forward supporting the therapy and developing an intuitive appreciation for the creative efforts shown in his life and in his dreams. The path forward must be travelled carefully, slowly, without the greed for "accomplishment", and accepting the limits that continue to announce themselves.

From our study of antiquity (Bergmann, 1992; Davoine & Gaudillière, 2004; Girard, 1977) and of the literature of *Don Quixote* and the *Iliad*, we have identified two primary modes of therapeutic engagement that emerge when working with traumatised and compromised resistant patients. In the *regressive mode* the therapeutic process is organised around the idea of the therapist serving as the "scapegoat surrogate" (Girard, 1977) who accepts the patient's projected guilt and shame and mistakenly believes that her "sacrificial" efforts can lead the subject towards some resolution of the trauma of his childhood. Here guilt distorts her empathy and the paranoid-schizoid patient seeks to transform the cooperative nature of the alliance with the master–slave dichotomy where she is overwhelmed and subordinated to his will (Nietzsche, 1994). The patient, still in the grasp of the trauma and madness of his childhood seeks to control the therapist as he was controlled by the figures of care that abandoned him. The patient's transitory evacuation of the bad into the therapist allows him to experience momentary innocence and relief and to use his narcissism and scorn to hold the therapist at bay as helpless, worthless, and a fraud. The treatment is sacrificed to the delusion of purification that is the imagined outcome of the scapegoat ritual offering.

The second form of the clinical relationship is a *progressive mode* where the boundaries and rules of the frame are maintained and where a therapeutic partnership is allowed to evolve that offers the patient the participation of the therapist as *"therapon"* (Davoine & Gaudillière, 2004, p. 150). This term, taken from the Greek, finds its most famous application in the *Iliad* where Patroclus is *therapon* to Achilles. *Therapon* means agent, representative, attendant, caretaker, and second-in-command, and this figure is the "keeper of the mind" (Shay, 1994, p. 44) of the master or warrior colleague. His job is to assist but not to replace. In the *Iliad*, Patroclus, in seeking to protect Achilles from the shame of his retreat from Agamemnon's greed and scorn, takes over his identity (wears his armour) and takes up the challenge of battle with the mighty Hector. Here he exceeds the role of the *therapon* and brings about the tragedy of his death and the scorn of the Trojans. Thus, in his confusion and manic response, Patroclus becomes the scapegoat for Achilles and brings about the crisis of Achaean leadership. He is killed and Achilles goes berserk with guilt and shame and engages in an orgy of murder and destruction.

In *Don Quixote* (Cervantes, 2005), the figure of Sancho Panza is a better *therapon* than Protroclus is to Achilles. He assists the Don in his mercurial adventures but does not take his place and does not impose his standards and goals upon the Don. His role as loyal second-in-command remains constant and he does not violate the implicit contract that holds the Don's values and goals as primary. Likewise Sancho Panza feels the agony when Don Quixote suffers the repetition of the failure of his many impossible dreams but he is not moved to exceed his role. The therapist in the role of the *therapon* is challenged to find the balance point between caring for the traumatised subject but remaining steadfast in her position and unwilling to offer the patient a form of help that defeats his essential dignity. She is a type of alter ego but always with the understanding that the subject must be supported so that he can cast off the illusions of his omnipotence and thus descend into the realm of the actual and the real. Progressive suffering emerges as meaning results from solving the problems of the past-in-the-present.

The humility of the *therapon* provides a sharp contrast with the grandiosity of the regressive hunger to use mythical–magical elements to make the impossible occur.

This book attempts to change the focus on treating an individual that Freud (1923b) described as suffering from a condition he termed the "*negative therapeutic reaction*" (p. 49, our emphasis). His hypothesis focused on his drive theory and the ways in which his speculative idea of the death instinct overwhelmed the patient's self and corrupted his superego, producing a measure of unconscious guilt that overwhelms the subject's ego and makes it impossible for him to participate in the treatment. The subject, unable to participate in the treatment, lapses into a masochistic process of self-abuse as the price to be paid for his sins and crimes and creates an intractable and inaccessible barrier of resistance that Freud (1937c, p. 252) felt was beyond the power of the psychoanalytic method to transform.

Our view presents a matrix of ideas that focuses upon the subject's loss of connection to the primal object of attachment, the internal figure of the mother and the resulting psychic collapse that presents him with a melancholic condition that compels him to create an internal ideal god-object to be used as a fetish replacement figure. The subject's retrospective construction of an internal realm of a "private religion" (Freud, 1907b, p. 119), validated and renewed through the use of the ritual of "sacrificial scapegoats" (Girard, 1977), provides the delusion that he is not alone, abandoned, and helpless. He operates in an order of traumatic compensation where the suffering of others in his stead can maintain his sense of omnipotence and acts as a barrier against his isolated and frustrating existence that threatens to drive him ever closer to madness or suicide. Rather than judging him as stubborn or obnoxious or pathologically masochistic, we present this subject as suffering from the tragedy of his disconnected emotional experience. The frustration and hopelessness he evokes in the therapist's experience of attempting to treat him, the painfully high price he pays through his suffering and sacrifice, may be reframed as the frantic activity of a lost subject of an imagined desperate "religion" that may be the path forward in treating such a tragic and traumatised human being.

CHAPTER ONE

Trauma, resistance, and sacrifice

Charles Ashbach

Statement of the problem

In the introduction to this book we profiled a particular type of patient who seeks psychotherapy or psychoanalysis and presents as motivated, intelligent, and eager for help but after a seemingly successful introductory phase, where work seems to get done and the treatment and alliance seem to unfold in a positive way, we come to recognise this individual is decidedly constrained by some inner force or experience causing him difficulty in the access to his emotions, memories, and associations. His associations are anything but free and the material soon reveals a limited range, and though he is pleasant and appears cooperative the sessions do not bring forth a feeling of alive engagement. His description of his problem or the statement of his goals for the treatment is vague. He moves carefully within the sessions, revealing a generally defensive attitude protecting some element of his experience, especially his pride, and treating the therapy as a danger that needs to be managed and controlled.

The treatment continues but the work does not deepen and we feel held at bay. It is clear that he wants something, something important, but he reacts as if he does not possess the skill to communicate the emotional experience that is his reason for being in the treatment in the first place. Though intelligent, his emotional language is by and large flat or mechanical and his difficulties or hesitations increase our hunger to find the means to help release him from his shell. As our frustration grows we often become more active or impatient to help him find the right word or a helpful association. Of course the countertransference becomes increasingly problematic as we become agitated that our skills and intuition aren't enough to set the experience going.

The person does not seem obviously ill, broken, or depressed but the inhibitions blocking his speech and the communication of his emotions suggest he is operating under a burden that stops him from telling us his story. In some cases he might become more obviously defiant, arrogant, or condescending and be more interested in observing us as we wrestle with *our* problems rather than finding a way to understand *his*. Thus, the patient announces in either a benign or aggressive form the burden of encountering this overwhelming problem. Or is it an intentional choice? Whatever the answer he seems unable to free himself from the self-defeating ambivalence that leaves him chronically miserable and filled with despair.

A critical advance in the understanding of the problem of intense resistance was provided by Freud with his study of "Mourning and melancholia" (1917e), where he showed that in the condition of the loss of a primary object the subject regresses to a deep unconscious dimension where he is able to recreate, in an imaginary and delusional form, the lost figure of attachment. The subject uses aspects of his own narcissism to both identify with the lost object and from it to fashion the replacement figure of the ideal (Steiner, 2005). This replacement figure enables him to both "be" and "have" the object and in this way he is protected against (denies) the loss and uses the magic of his omnipotence to fend off feelings of helplessness and collapse. The narcissistic element of this transformed object provides the delusion that he is one with it, fused and inseparable and therefore does not have to contend with the horrifying demands of loss, grief, regret, and mourning. His identification with the ideal figure fuels his feelings of power and enables him to decrease his contact with the actual, external object world, leads to omnipotent thinking, decreases his encounter with reality testing, and, most importantly, increases the conflict between wishing to be alive in one's object relationships or to be "at one with one's dead internal objects" (Ogden, 2002, p. 767), thus increasing the danger of suicide.

The patient hides his aggression against his objects by unconsciously heaping upon himself the displaced attacks against the lost love object. His self-abuse is in part a camouflage protecting his ego against the attacks and condemnation of his conscience and he feels perfectly entitled to express his displeasure without the slightest sign of humility; he is comfortable presenting himself as the victim. As Ogden says, the subject expresses his sense of "injustice" incessantly, but eventually his superego causes him to be "crushed" and he accepts his fate as punishment for his crime of driving the object away (Ogden, 2002, p. 772). It is this experience of ambivalence that causes the subject to be caught in an oscillating emotional space that allows for no pleasure and no peace.

So we are confronted with the irony that Freud in "Mourning and melancholia" (1917e) presented an object relations understanding of resistance using the central event of object loss and in *The Ego and the Id* (1923b) presented his formal theory of resistance based upon the impact of drive conflict focused around the impact of the death drive (1920g). He attempted to explain the patient's problem, which he described as the subject's "negative therapeutic reaction" (NTR) as caused by the distortions in the subject's superego and his inability to bear up under the impact of unbearable guilt. In this model the drive, actually the impact of unconscious guilt, makes the subject withdraw from the treatment process and use sadomasochistic acting out as a means of punishment to pay the price for his sins. This approach led to no further development and was eventually surpassed by developments in object relations thinking.

Thesis

The purpose of this chapter is to demonstrate that we can achieve a radically improved understanding of a patient's chronic resistance if we apply Freud's model of mind (1917e), articulated in "Mourning and melancholia", to understand the ways in which the subject's mind has been crushed, disturbed, and disorganised by the traumatic and catastrophic loss of his primal object. The following elements are central:

1. The "primitive agonies" (Winnicott, 1974) unleashed by this loss trigger a desperate process of magical, narcissistic restoration that culminates in the creation of an ideal figure of love and connection

(Steiner, 2005) that is the delusional substitute (replacement) for the lost actual object. Ogden's observation frames the impact on the subject of such a phantasmic, manic, and self-generated inner world: "[A] fantasied unconscious object world replaces an actual external one; omnipotence replaces helplessness; immortality substitutes for the uncompromising realities of the passage of time and death; triumph replaces despair; contempt substitutes for love" (2002, pp. 777–778).

2. The patient's regression causes him to experience a register of narcissistic, unconscious experience that enables him to activate a primitive sadomasochistic fantasy that his suffering and pain are the means for him to acquire gratification, forgiveness, and omnipotent power.

3. The splitting of the self leads to a dissociated "double self" (Wurmser, 2007, p. 11) where self-idealisation, perfection, and purity are active in one sector and the subject's enormous feelings of hatred, envy, and revenge exist in another. The problem of "owning" or taking responsibility for one's desires and actions cannot be said to coalesce under such fragmented circumstances.

4. The subject's extensive injuries compel him to seek to construct the treatment as a "stage" (setting) for the portrayal of his earliest battles and losses and for the disposal of his unbearable burden of guilt and shame. The treatment in such a form is often reduced to a process of constant conflict, disagreement, and injury until the decoding of the aggression and misunderstanding is solved.

5. The patient is a depressed individual operating in a register of regressed, omnipotent, and narcissistic unconsciousness that seeks to transform the treatment from a psychological process of investigation, insight, and understanding into a "private religion" (Freud, 1907b) by co-opting the ritualistic and ceremonial aspects of the treatment. He seeks to bring about a process of suffering and sacrifice occurring in a "sacred" order of experience where he seeks to "offer up" the positive elements of his life—his talents, accomplishments, hopes, and relationships—on the altar of the treatment in order to receive, in return, the bounty of his imagined god-object. His ego remains in control, now operating within the shadow of his imagined, omnipotent god-object and this form of treatment is a perversion of the dynamism and generativity of the actual process of therapy as it cancels out the need for the acceptance of loss, grief, guilt, and mourning. The "new life" of the patient, the therapeutic

child of the treatment (Chasseguet-Smirgel, 1985a) cannot be born because the subject's fusion with his "ideal" delusional object destroys the power of the primal couple. The patient's dependency remains centred on the idealised version of himself hidden within the god-object that he directs his sacrifices to. The acknowledgement of the loss of the prime object and his acceptance of a new "libidinal position" of his relationship with the therapist (Freud, 1917e, p. 244) is fought and the success of the treatment hangs in the balance.

The path to achieve this new perspective on resistance is by relating the connections between trauma, the breakdown of the self, and the construction of a new self inside the register of suffering and sacrifice.

Trauma, breakdown, and the "new" self

Trauma is the force that crushes the self, overturns the order of the internal realm, and transforms the subject's expectations of the external world into an ominous and dangerous place; it drives the subject back into a fantasy world of wish and magic and makes the possibility of belief in human beings a difficult and risky challenge. It is the starting point to understand chronic and intense resistance.

> So a traumatic event is one that, for a particular individual, breaks through or overrides the discriminatory, filtering process, and overrides any temporal denial or patch-up of the damage. The mind is flooded with a kind and degree of stimulation that is far more than it can make sense of or manage. Something very violent feels as though it has happened internally, and this mirrors the violence that is felt to have happened, or indeed has actually happened, in the external world. There is a massive disruption in functioning, amounting to a kind of breakdown. … It leaves the individual vulnerable to intense and overwhelming anxieties from internal sources as well as from the actual external events. (Garland, 1998, p. 10–11)

The concept of trauma—from the Greek for wound, hurt, or defeat—has become so ubiquitous, used so casually for so many events, that it is near-saturated. Trauma as I use it defines an emotional and psychic catastrophe that envelops the self, rattles the soul, rips something whole into tragic pieces, and, as Garland says, "breaks through" and "overrides" the filters protecting the self and leads to a "massive disruption … amounting to a kind of breakdown". Here Winnicott's (1974) characterisation of the subject's "primitive agonies" bears repeating: a return to an unintegrated state; falling forever; depersonalisation and loss of capacity to relate to objects, with a regression into an autistic or primitive mental state (1974, p. 104). Winnicott says that where the repressed catastrophe is not addressed, the treatment is in the grip of a collusion, a belief in a neurotic enterprise, and this leads nowhere because the problem is located in a psychotic register of inner experience. Movement in the face of such resistance requires the engagement of the "main issue", to be able to approach and "experience" the thing feared, in the transference, which is the breakdown (1974, p. 105). It is this catastrophe, waiting to be experienced, that is at the centre of the tragically resistant patient.

Trauma gives rise to a sense of total helplessness in the face of clashing emotions, triggers the fantasy of omnipotence, and entails the hope for a magical transformation of self and world. Efforts towards conflict resolution fail leading to the constant repetition of the problem. Emotions and fantasies are global and out of control and are irreconcilable with each other but the self is driven to impose some measure of control on them; frequently this "control" shows up as addictive, compulsive, and perverse sexuality and behaviours that remind the subject that he is not in control of his life.

The subject's splitting and fragmentation results in the confusing experience of a dissociated "doubleness" (Wurmser, 2007, p. 11) that enables him to protect himself against the experience of breakdown by occupying different registers of experience. Davoine and Gaudillière (2004, p. xxvii) observe that the impact of trauma as a "powerful blow that actually took place" (a real external event) has ejected the subject out of the space–time coordinates of his life into a "zone of nonexistence" where time has been immobilised; he seeks to find some means of finding his way back to the moment where his time and his experience of being as he knew it ceased to exist. The patient is being pushed by an invisible event possessing substantial emotional gravity that attempts to use conflict, difference, and disagreement to find memory or create recognition through a scene that might enable some element of the trauma to come into being. In this way transference "difficulties" can be understood as the only means available for the tragically resistant subject to inscribe his lost meanings into the fabric of the treatment.

Of course, there are many forms of trauma and each possesses the power to fracture and crush the self and hold the subject in a state of suspended animation. Wurmser's definition enables us to consider the types that can drive the subject into his psychic retreat of intractable resistance.

> I do not mean "trauma" in a trivial, universalized way, but in the sense of events with life-altering severity, intensity and usually repetitiveness, like the killing of the mother by the father, repeated severe operations in early childhood, massive fighting between the parents, sexual abuse and other forms of physical mistreatment, but also some severe intersubjective harm, like chronic humiliation and systematic squashing of all individuality by "soul blindness" and "soul murder". (2007, p. 6)

In my examination of the histories of my most resistant patients the one common element that stood out was the subject's deeply confusing and inordinately frustrating experience of being cared for by a mother "who remains alive but is, so to speak, psychically dead in the eyes of the young child in her care", the figure that Green (1986, p. 142) termed the "dead mother". While other, more dramatic types of trauma have occurred (accidents, surgery, family violence) it has been this less "visible" trauma that seems to have had the most impact on the regressed patient.

It is this figure of apparent "love, care and attention" trapped in a bereavement of her own having to do with the loss of a primary love figure (parent, spouse, sibling, or other child) that causes her to operate in the painfully confusing register of being both "dead and alive" that subjects her child to "severe intersubjective harm", which I describe as traumatic. As Green describes her, this mother:

> has been constituted in the child's mind, following maternal depression, brutally transforming a living object, which was a source of vitality for the child, into a distant figure, toneless, practically inanimate ... Thus, the dead mother ... is a mother who remains alive but who is, so to speak, psychically dead in the eyes of the young child in her care. (Green, 1986, p. 142)

Green observes (1986, p. 146) that this loss for the child is not bloody, as in castration anxiety, but bears the "colours" of mourning—black or white—and is the consequence of a "blank" anxiety which expresses a loss that has been experienced on a narcissistic level. Here we discover

Freud's earlier observation in describing the melancholic patient (1917e) that his link to the object was limited and secondary, a "shadow". Thus the loss of the mother in such a paradoxical and confusing situation evokes a series of reactions that Green describes as blank anxiety, blank mourning, negative hallucination, and blank psychosis and leads to the problem of emptiness or the emergence of the negative (1986, p. 146) as a central dynamic feature of the patient's problem. Here the patient's deadening and lifeless withdrawal points to the tragedy of why he would choose to exclude himself from the treatment process and, more poignantly, from life itself so as not to re-experience the catastrophe of his barely recognised but continually felt loss. The patient's tragic resistance understood through the lens of the "dead mother" matrix offers the therapist a greater capacity for empathy and containment and helps protect against joining him in his hopelessness and deadness.

This "dead mother" situation presents a complex and paradoxical scene that enfolds the patient in its turbulence. The mother has been "lost", captured in the psychic–emotional circumstances of her bereavement but continues to be bodily present to her child as she attends to his *outside* and the job of managing his material comforts is retained. She is both present and absent, though a more emotional way to consider it, following Bion (1965, p. 107), is to describe her as an "active no-thing". She is the "shadow" cast by the mother she might have been and continues to act on the subject as a type of ghost figure. Here we might think of her as a kind of "zombie" mother who is both dead and alive in an emotionally bizarre and terrifying form.

As McDougall (1980, p. 252) points out, psychic suffering at this early phase is "indistinguishable" from physical suffering and thus these painful and crushing experiences are often taken up in a physiological form (unrepresented beta elements, Bion, 1962) and determine many patients' psychosomatic and addictive difficulties. As Davoine and Gaudillière (2004, p. 12) point out, where the patient experiences such a powerful experience there is often no conscious memory or representation of the actual events he received from that blank, empty, or dead mother and accordingly he cannot communicate his experience through words. In such cases the patient makes use of an "inscription", a type of emotionally powerful, projective identification to "communicate" his experience to, or more correctly *into*, the being of the therapist in the hope of establishing a connection that might lead to the development of a meaning.

And as importantly, the "dead mother" projectively exudes a constant signal of distress, pain, and tragedy that binds her child to her. Though she is generally elsewhere she nonetheless desperately needs her child to contain the unbearable, split-off realities that make her experience so saturated with grief and bereavement, and thus a constant circuit of projected internal objects from the mother are used to gain ever deeper access to the privacy of the child's self. Though it may not be expressed with the drama of "soul murder" (Shengold, 1989), it is nonetheless a ruthlessly powerful form of trauma and personality invasion. Thus, from a split-off aspect of his unconscious the child is forced to become a witness to the tragedy of her life. The patient's subsequent attempt to communicate his plight involves the elements of "her plight" that leads to confusion and inarticulateness. A double-bind response emerges in him: on the one side to flee or destroy her; and on the other to become the heroic figure of rescue and salvation that seeks to repair the grave damage affecting her. This feeling, experienced as a compulsion to repair the mother, is at the centre of Klein's (1935) "depressive position" and adds an additional dimension to the problem of dealing with the lost object. The patient not only is tasked with replacing her in his psyche but now the job of repairing her to an impossible position of wellbeing complicates the patient's experience further and adds to motivation of wanting relief without having to understand his challenges.

Where the subject has been subjected to the intense and sadistic forces of his mother's or of the family's frustrated and overwhelming pathology, there is born in him the experience of being a prisoner in a "totalitarian family ambience" that Jarrell (1962, p. 146) calls "one of God's concentration camps". This experience often leads to a deep feeling that the subject has been exposed to "the deliberate attempt to eradicate or compromise the separate identity of another person" (Shengold, 1989, p. 4), and in response there grows in him an absolute intention of retaliating against this monstrous and overwhelming figure that is supposed to be a figure of love. Thus subject and object become fused, forced together through the mad extremes of love and hate, and the subject is now "possessed" by the Other with his soul in "bondage to someone else" (Shengold, 1989, p. 2). In this way the patient's resistance seems to be a last, desperate opportunity to rework the psychotic, psychopathic moment when his subjectivity was taken from him and often such a hope is greater than his desire for freedom and liberation. In this way the patient (child) is tied to the object within the mad paradox of wanting to destroy this figure and at the same time committed to her rescue and repair—what Ogden (2002, p. 767) describes as a state of "mutual captivity".

The ancillary experiences of the child in this situation, in addition to the feelings of emptiness, confusion, and frustration include feelings of guilt, shame, and self-condemnation, reflecting the overwhelming sense of his "omnipotence of responsibility" (Wurmser & Jarass, 2013a, p. 13) for somehow having caused the maddeningly vague problem that consumes his mother. This "imagined" power reflects the child's naive sense that he is the centre of the world and all events occurring there are his absolute responsibility, and thus he dreads being attached to another because he must assume such a central role. At the same time, on another level of consciousness, he harbours deeply buried experiences of frustration and anger at having to remain chronically at the "edge" of his mother's world, forced to function as a satellite with no means to gain access to her centre, her warmth, and her protection. This patient is often described as anxious, worried, or obsessional but from my clinical experience he is better appreciated if we recognise how he struggles to fend off the shadow of his "breakdown" that continues to exert its signal of "blank anxiety" that allows for no relief and no understanding.

Considering the various elements of trauma, the vague but pressing compulsions to both rescue and attack the mother, the feelings of guilt and shame regarding the subject's responsibility for the mother's situation lead to his withdrawal into a very intricate psychic retreat (Steiner, 1993) where he builds a position, a regressive container, more like a claustrum that is part crypt and part fortress and seeks to keep the world at bay as he considers his options for both protection and for engagement. His confusion revolves around the contradiction that he is both the lost and helpless child as well as the responsible party for rescuing and reviving the maternal object. His emotions are extreme and his abilities to act are both unappreciated and narcissistically overstated. The key element in considering this patient is his deficiency in thinking (Bion, 1997) and his inability to make contact with his "inaccessible unconscious" (Civitarese, 2013) where the elements of basic and primitive memory are stored. As Civitarese says, the therapeutic task is to seek through intersubjective links and connections, discovered through the act of reverie in the analytic field (Civitarese, 2008), the means to gain access to the negative areas of the mind in order to produce transformations in the (resistant) patient.

The subject's masochistic attacks against himself lead to a profoundly reduced capacity to enjoy himself and the pleasures of life and reveals itself as a decided condition of anhedonia. When he is driven to enjoy pleasure, by pent up desire, he takes it as a "challenge" or job or is able to experience pleasure only in an altered state of consciousness, specifically through the use of drugs and alcohol; or his pleasures, because of the superego pressures, are experienced in a perverse register of excitement, mortification, and pain.

The lurking object of the damaged mother

Freud's (1917e) explanation of the problem of depression (melancholia) and my utilisation of it to link to the problems of resistance and sacrifice requires an additional element to complete the complex dynamic picture that is the core of the patient's intense resistance. Melanie Klein (1935) took Freud's nascent ideas around the concept of internal objects ("On narcissism", 1914c; "Mourning and melancholia", 1917e) and developed a complex and elegant system of internal object relations that was founded upon her understanding of the mind as passing through two basic positions; the earliest and most primitive she termed the paranoid–schizoid position and emphasised its split nature with a division of the world into good and bad. Further development under the impact of the loving mother led to the integration of the subject's perceptions, thoughts, and internal objects that occurred during the depressive position, so named because as the child integrated his objects and experience he felt sad and depressed upon realising the object that he hated and attacked was the same object that he admired and loved. Klein considered this depressive position to be equal to Freud's concept of the Oedipus complex as a central point of consolidation in the development of the human personality in health and in pathology.

Freud's (1917e) understanding of object loss emphasised how the subject replaced the actual lost object with a self-constructed phantasy object to deny the loss and to have a figure of love and perfection that was under the exclusive control of the subject. We can say, following Freud's formulation, that this "ideal" replacement object functions as a "fetish" object (Freud, 1927e, p. 150) to cover over the missing reality of the primary figure of attachment. Freud said that depression emerges because the replacement figure does not restore the lost integrity of the relationship between the subject and his mother. Klein's scheme (1935) of the depressive position points up the problem of the subject caught in a double bind circumstance regarding such a loss. On one hand he works to attack and punish the object for its absence and abandonment and on the other he is driven by a fundamental instinctual response, a primal unconscious directive that seeks to bring about the object's repair and restoration in order for the subject to feel that the primary relationship has been re-established on a foundation of fullness, contentment, and love. The implication of the depressive position is that the subject cannot integrate his ego and self if the primary, internal object is in a state of damage or injury. This dynamic situation implies that underneath the ambivalent conflict between love and hate that emerges in the treatment is a deeper and more profound challenge the subject has to face and resolve. He must confront the dreaded issue of having injured or damaged the primary maternal figure, as a function of his feeling of his omnipotence of responsibility (Wurmser, 2007, p. 1) and must act in some profound and consequential way to repair, or if possible to restore, the object to its imagined state of perfection, beauty, and completeness. The goal of perfect restoration is an impossible phantasy but the subject presses on with this task so that he will be able to purify himself of the guilt, shame, and moral responsibility that is the consequence of his unconscious states of aggression, greed, envy, and retribution.

Klein's paper on the depressive position and the internal objects involved was published in 1935, the year after her son Hans died in a mountain climbing accident. Joan Riviere, a close ally and disciple of Klein, published a profound paper (1936/1991) on the problem of the "negative therapeutic reaction", and its relationship to loss and the problems of reparation. In that work she provides a dramatic description of the emotional and existential crisis that emerges when the subject feels responsible for the catastrophe of the object's damage or loss. She speaks of the way that a primitive form of the superego, a paranoid–schizoid version, attacks the subject with a persecutory form of depression and links this dynamic circumstance with the patient's intense reaction of opposition and resistance.

> The content of the depressive position … is the situation in which all one's loved ones *within* are dead and destroyed, all goodness is dispersed, lost, in fragments, wasted and scattered to the winds; nothing is left *within* but utter desolation. (Riviere, 1936/1991, p. 144, original emphasis)

The patient's anxiety is so great because "life hangs by a hair and at any moment the situation of full horror may be realised." The patient, at the core of his unconscious, fears "death or madness, his own and others', is ever before the eyes of his unconscious mind" (ibid., p. 145). Further, she provides the link to explain the patient's lack of engagement: "I think the patient's fear of *being forced to death by the analysis* is one of the major underlying factors in this type of resistant case" (original emphasis). By stopping the movement of the treatment, by freezing time, by fending off the therapist's goodwill and empathy he seeks to "keep things going ... and postpones the crash, the day of reckoning and judgment" (ibid.). In general we can say that few therapists are aware the patient fears being "forced to death by the analysis" and we are always at risk of overwhelming him if we continue in our therapeutic "zeal" to seek progress or success in the treatment when we have not discovered the magnitude of the crisis that substantiates the patient's intense experience of resistance.

The patient "refuses to get better himself" until his primary internal object is completely repaired and he maintains a manic system of defence against losing control of the treatment. He is pitched back and forth between saving himself and saving the object, with the ultimate consideration driving him to place the fate of the object before that of the self, for there is no life without the existence of the object. As Riviere points out (1936/1991, p. 151) it is "the patient's love for his internal objects which lies behind and produces the unbearable guilt and pain, the need *to sacrifice* his life for theirs, and so the prospect of death, that makes the resistance so stubborn" (my emphasis). Confronted by the patient's divided battle between intense, devotional love and furious and violent revenge we recognise the forms of manic defence the subject deploys to protect himself against the recognition of his intense, unconscious emotions and fantasies of need and attachment.

Fairbairn (1952, p. 65) speaks of the subject's need in conditions of conflict and loss to take the "bad" element of the parents on to himself. As Fairbairn observes: "the child would rather be bad himself than to have bad objects." This he terms the child's "moral defence" and emphasises the child's intense dependency needs that are protected through such a manoeuvre. The child's internalisation of the bad obtains a measure of external security through giving up a good deal of his own feelings of internal security. The similarity with Riviere's position is that the child "remakes" the parents, repairs them, and takes the burden of badness on his shoulders. Riviere goes on to say (ibid., p. 151): "What is underneath is a love (a craving for absolute bliss in complete union with a perfect object for ever and ever) and this love is bound up with an uncontrollable and insupportable fury of disappointment." Here she identifies the patient's goal as wanting to not only restore the object to its imagined grandeur but to establish it as the permanent figure of infantile love and attachment with no requirement to separate and mourn her passing. Understood from this perspective, the patient's resistance provides him with the means to "stop time", to reverse the threat of the future, and to be able to keep open the door to the past. It is this lurking dimension of the primary object, beyond its presence or absence, that confuses the treatment and calls upon the therapist's recognition of the object at the core of the patient's psyche.

Further elements of resistance

James Grotstein (1979), in his study of borderline and psychotic patients, identified a cluster of psychic elements where splitting and fragmentation and the unbearable agony of confusion and guilt has led to a particular "sleight-of-hand", where the subject is able to "disavow his own existence" and become not just "omnipotent but invisible" (ibid., p. 411). This action is taken to evade the "laws of chance" so that he cannot be held accountable and "compelled to experience" the tragedy, of the loss of the object and the obliteration of his world (context) that he believes he caused. The subject's negation of himself produces an inner self that becomes more and more omnipotent and critical of "itself" and others and takes up a position of pure negation so that he cannot be trapped by a "cryptic and sinister force" possessing "omnipotent and ominous authority" (ibid., p. 414). We might say, at a deeper level his ability to negate, to use his ultimate position of No!, is his primary weapon of defence and also his primary object of addiction and we are advised to move carefully in trying to understand the magical power he ascribes to his No! if we are to remain outside the realm of his hopelessness and omnipotence.

Part of the patient's agony is his experience that the good offered by the therapist is a kind of tormenting and sadistic trick. His hunger for the help and understanding of the treatment pulls him desperately towards the therapist, in a state of manic greed, but his memories of so many painful frustrations and disappointments lead him to cynically dismiss the therapist's offer of understanding and containment. He feels intense envy towards the object and to protect against being trapped in a nightmare of unending gratitude and dependency seeks to devalue, mock, degrade, and dismiss the object as unimportant, perverse, or corrupt. These extreme inner self-states that might seem emergent in only the most bizarre cases actually constitute a state of "personal hell" experienced by the most intensely resistant and oppositional patients. Because their scorn and negation exert such a powerful force against the world, they view this power as a "personal asset"—what one patient described as "my psychic spine".

Sacrifice

An anthropological understanding of sacrifice finds its crucial importance consists in granting the group or community the means for uniting the collective into a common purpose with a common set of shared and binding assumptions. "All become one" through a religious ideal and the ritualistic, sacrificial experience that enables each member to be bound to the collective through the compelling emotional experience of faith, aggression, and awe. When the group becomes saturated with powerful internal tensions, feuds, and rivalries and when violence breaks out, one prime social function is to provide the group the necessary mechanism to evacuate the destabilising forces. The prime means for this in antiquity was the use of "scapegoat sacrifice" (Girard, 1977), which used non-aligned and unrepresented subjects (slaves, prisoners of war, hapless wanderers) to absorb the anxieties and dangers that such forces produced. When the group lost a battle, or a crop, or the purity of the community through infestation it turned to its leaders and priests to purify the elements that had invaded the community and the destruction of a scapegoat figure was offered to the group deity employing its mythic–ritual customs and figures to "pay for" the sin or failure that was assumed to exist at the centre of the group's problem.

In the Introduction to this book we used Bergmann's (1992) classification to identify the primitive form of group life where the deity was created to contain the violence and ferocity of the membership reflecting the primitive (paranoid–schizoid) nature of the superego of the group. In groups so organised the faithful atone for their "sins and guilt" through the propitiating action of a murderous sacrifice, that is, the killing of an alive and valuable object, originally a child, within the structure of the collective's religious belief. The scapegoat's sacred destruction allows for the members of the community to experience relief and purgation through the "smoke from the altars" and the requisitioning of "slaughtered flesh" (Girard, 1977, p. 7). The scapegoat, though innocent in fact, is guilty in the mythology of the community, and his destruction allows for momentary relief experienced by the group. No lasting transformation occurred, but the community kept an inventory of such tragic figures on hand to be utilised whenever the tensions in the collective reached dangers levels. The Greek word for scapegoat is *pharmakos*, which links up with the modern, American idea to take a pill whenever stress or conflict threatens to overwhelm the self.

Following the paradigm presented describing the role of sacrifice in the life of groups when they are in a state of distress, we can say that the tragically resistant and regressed patient operates as a primitive group of one. When the patient experiences stress, anxiety, or terror associated with his emotional and relational life and is unable to make sense of reflecting some element of his personality, he seeks to engage a ceremonial means for controlling his experience. The goal is to organise himself maintaining a narcissistic component at the centre of his personality to provide him with the idea that he can continue to experience himself as both good and loving. Thus, his participation in the act of scapegoat sacrifice must provide him the means to obscure his violence and arrogance from the awareness of his superego. Maintaining the ceremonial metaphor of the primitive sacrifice, we can say the patient has two paths before him. In the one approach he is both the high priest of his "private religion" (Freud, 1907b) as well as the scapegoat surrogate being offering up to atone for the sin that has broken his world apart. The self-aspects to be offered up are those judged to be weak, pathetic, vulnerable, and terrified and he assigns complete responsibility to this sacrificial figure, and ruthlessly and sadistically attacks him. Bion (1962) describes such evacuation as the subject's evasion of guilt and responsibility due to the violence and sadism of his superego. He is unable to mentalize these elements and can only use the unconscious process of projective identification to evacuate the superego judgements and anxiety associated with guilt and shame and thus relieve the unbearable moral pressure.

Or he can be the high priest of the sacrificial ritual, with the therapist recruited to act as the scapegoat figure enduring the burdens of guilt, shame, and blame for the injuries and failures that have occurred in the patient's life. As one patient said: "I do alright in life by and large but when I come here the problems occur." In both versions a central aspect of the patient remains identified with the omnipotent, narcissistic figure of the ideal object and this connection is vital because it provides the illusion that the subject is protected against the traumatic dangers of discovery and moral condemnation of his primitive superego. When the therapist becomes the sacrificial figure of the patient's hate and aggression it is common for her to experience feelings of insecurity, doubt, and low self-esteem as she is loaded with the failures that the patient deploys against himself. In this moment of countertransference confusion the patient has "reversed roles" (Bion, 1965) with the therapist, who is invited to climb upon the "altar" of the treatment where she can pay for her "sins" as failed caregiver.

Wurmser describes the human mind as containing a complex of primal fantasies and schemes that emerge from the unconscious to provide a way of making sense of the complexities of human experience especially in times of stress and regression. One primary fantasy at work in the subject's use of sacrifice is the masochistic experience of pain bringing about the transformation of the world through the agency of a supernatural figure:

> By my suffering I transform suffering into pleasure, anxiety into sexual excitement, hatred into love, separation into fusion, helplessness into power and revenge, guilt into forgiveness (and) shame into triumph. (Wurmser, 2007, p. 268)

This phantasy obliterates the need for separation, for dependency, for honesty and vulnerability. It magically reverses the problems of hate and turns them into the benefits of love and, most importantly, one does not feel the terrible burden of responsibility and pain of guilt for one's choices and acts. Novick and Novick (1991, p. 324) comment, in their study of depressed–masochistic patients, how the subject holds a deep and often religious conviction of a "delusion of omnipotence" that "pain is the magical means by which all wishes are gratified, and pain justifies the omnipotent hostility and revenge contained in the masochistic fantasy." Such patients seek to create a "sacrifice" by making a deal with "God or the Devil" (some omnipotent, supernatural power) so that a precious person in their life, generally a frustrating intimate figure, might be saved from the unconscious destructiveness felt by the patient.

The pressures involved in the sacrificial process also distort the challenges of the oedipal complex and the subject's problems of aggression towards the father figure as he seeks to reconcile the intricate path between parricide and identification. The necessity of having to "kill" the father (parricide), psychically, that is, to grow and separate from him and thus gain emancipation, autonomy, and authority and then to replace him through identification (Loewald, 1979, p. 390), becomes distorted and perverted because the subject is not adequately consolidated in his identity relative to the maternal object. In such a case the subject is unable to mourn his experience of the crisis of separation and becomes trapped in an "inexhaustible" process of sacrificial punishment. Repression then takes over and he is confronted with a troubling unconscious attitude of passive and excessively dependent clinging that marks a pathological development. Here we see the challenges of the interpenetration of the depressive position (Klein, 1935) with the oedipal complex and can appreciate the consequences of traumatic object loss.

Mental pain versus psychic suffering

Bion (1970, p. 19) differentiated *mental pain* from *psychic suffering* and observed that mental pain was an experience trapped within the body, unavailable to the symbolic transformation of alpha function (Bion, 1962), which could not be tolerated and remained isolated as a thing-in-itself and therefore suitable only for evacuation. Paul Koehler (on p. 87) (Chapter Three, this volume) points out that the word suffer means "to carry", with the implication that the psychic factor necessary to transform pain into suffering is the subject's capacity for "toleration", the ability to tolerate the crisis, frustration, and madness of the experience without destroying the link connecting the body and the mind. Here we anticipate the necessity of the therapist's containment to support the patient as he struggles to express something—a sound, a memory, a colour—that might suggest a link to the experience embedded in the pain. Lombardi (2016) focuses on the subtlety and importance of bodily feelings that might contain links that could offer connection to self-states previously blocked by dissociations. It is probably more accurate to think of the chronically resistant patient as suffering from a state of being that is "outside" the order of a body–mind connection and the therapy work gradually evolves into an attempt to "slow down" our engagement with the patient so the specifics of each moment might be encountered and made available to the reverie of the therapist and to the intersubjective experience of both parties in the treatment.

Davoine and Gaudillière (2004) speak about such patients reflecting the re-experience of previously unprocessed or represented states of traumatic experience that cannot be spoken but are unconsciously "inscribed", one might say chiselled into the tissues of the therapist's body or into the register of her intuition, and when the words are missing, the patient resorts to "showing" the therapist the total situation in which the trauma emerged. Here we recognise Freud's (1915a, p. 201) differentiation between "thing presentations" and "object representations". The psychic "thing" is felt as a literal and concrete presence existing in the unconscious, mind–body matrix, real as a dream is real but without a conscious, symbolic form to allow it to exist in the order of the psyche. A prime means for inscription is the staging of an enactment that seeks to embody the "thingness" of the patient's trauma in a kind of dimensional "passion play" where the intricacies of his traumatic life experience become revivified in the transference and ultimately become represented as "characters" (Ferro, 2013, p. 5), that is symbolic representations that can take their place in the patient's conscious narrative. As Sandler says (1976a), the subject seeks to "actualise" an unconscious internal object within the being of the therapist in the moment-by-moment unfolding of the transference. Thus, the many problems and issues that occupy the transference—arguments and resistances of all kinds—of time boundaries, bounced checks, confusion over missed appointments, and the innumerable opportunities for failures and misunderstandings—are each the dramatic context for staging the internal crisis, reflecting the system of internal objects of the patient's trauma.

Two therapeutic roles

Part of the challenge of working with a traumatised–resistant patient is to make contact with the operative level of psychic and emotional experience that characterises him in the session. From the preceding discussion of the difference between primitive mental pain and mature suffering we recognise two types or modes of psychic experience. In the *primitive mode* the subject experiences an intense emotional experience of pain, distress, and anxiety that acts against the ego's containment, limits or destroys the capacity for symbolic transformation, and leads to the search for relief through denial, evacuation, and enactments. Unable to make sense of his situation he seeks to reverse roles with the therapist and through a series of enactments and crises attempts to seduce and manipulate her into occupying the role of his helpless and overwhelmed infant/child self. The inversion of subject and object temporarily frees him from captivity by his pernicious and sadistic superego and he seeks to make the therapist experience the guilt, shame, and impotence that he was forced to experience in the original setting of his family. Activating a measure of manic narcissistic omnipotence enables him to look down on the therapist, consider her to be his scapegoat (Girard, 1977) that is under his control, and compel her to suffer on his behalf the traumatic burdens of his personality. In this way he feels that he can avoid the dark spectre of depression and his dread of isolated alienation.

In the *progressive mode* of containment, the therapist seeks to establish a particularly intricate balance with the traumatised patient recognising the contradictory nature of his split demands for fusion, identification, and access on the one side and emotional distance and schizoid impenetrability on the other. The therapist is continually challenged to appreciate the radically regressed nature of the subject's psychic experience and the primitive nature of the peril—existential dread that causes him to search for salvation and purification rather than "mere" understanding and insight. His projective intensity continually seeks to gain access to the "inside" of the therapist's experience and demands she become a participant in his psychic struggle, an actor in his "passion play" rather than simply a witness, as his psyche becomes extended to, and interpenetrating of, the total context of the treatment.

The patient's mode of communication operates outside of the normal channels of the spoken word and the therapist is continually tasked with the need to make sense of unusual memories, associations, and feeling states that emerge in relationship to this patient's sessions. He has the uncanny ability to make contact with most sensitive elements of the therapist's internal object system even when he appears to be distant or disinterested and in spite of the many difficulties the therapist experiences she is challenged to "participate" in the subject's experience of pain, misery, and madness in order to know his self-states from the inside out, as it were, while working to maintain the boundaries and symbolic functioning that are the core elements of her therapeutic action. This challenge necessitates a transitory distortion in her sense of self, a temporary loss of her identity that allows her to interpenetrate his regressed, traumatic experience so that she might 'host' the extreme states that will provide her with a deep knowledge of the trauma that drove the subject out of himself even when this process causes her to feel intense conditions of guilt and shame.

The countertransference that determines the therapeutic role established in relation to the patient is a by-product of the intensity of the subject's trauma and the extent to which archaic anxieties and unresolved inner conflicts in the therapist are activated. Where the intensity of the patient's experience draws upon traumatic experience and psychotic states, the therapist is faced with containing the catastrophic trauma experienced in the patient's development. When the patient chronically resists the therapist's efforts and care, she becomes threatened by depressive anxieties and guilt-feelings associated with her struggle to repair and restore the wellbeing of the primary object of her childhood. The ability to recognise and contain this set of interacting variables determines whether the therapist occupies the regressive role of the *sacrificial figure of the scapegoat* or the progressive figure that Davoine (2004) describes using the classic Greek term *therapon*, a figure of care, support, and dedication that is prepared to work relentlessly to assist his "master" but who knows his limits and protects himself from the confusion of exceeding his boundaries.

The term is taken from Homer's the *Iliad* (1998) and describes an individual who is servant, attendant, minister or "second in command" to a king, ruler, or lord. The subject has established a special bond of duty and responsibility for his "master" and seeks to provide vital support as that object faces the most difficult trials and challenges of his office. He is loyal, devoted, and steadfast, prepared to suffer in order to realise his goal of support. Two prime examples of the *therapon* are Patroclus in his relationship to Achilles during the battle for Troy and Sancho Panza as *therapon* to Don Quixote during his long quest to find the figure of Dulcinea.

At a crucial moment in the Trojan War Achilles becomes locked in a narcissistic battle with King Agamemnon over the possession of the prize slave girl, Briseis. She was granted to Achilles as tribute and symbol of his power and glory but Agamemnon, as King, claimed her for his own. Furious at this insult Achilles withdraws from the battle, causing the Greek army to languish in confusion. Patroclus as *therapon* to Achilles senses the growing danger of the dispirited army and dons Achilles' armour and rouses the Greek warriors to war frenzy. Initially successful, Patroclus is carried away with the thrill of power and prestige as he mimics his divine master and exceeds the limits of his role and intent. Now filled with hubris, ambition, and greed he turns away from the supportive nature of his task and decides to confront the mighty Trojan warrior Hector and in that moment seeks to *replace* Achilles and fight his battle for him. Patroclus is not prepared for such a battle, has lost sight of his identity, and has turned away from his subordinate role as *therapon*. Hector immediately recognises the deception and kills Patroclus. In this way we observe the consequences when the *therapon* exceeds the boundaries of his role and in attempting to exceed his limits and task becomes a helpless sacrificial scapegoat.

The second *therapon* figure is Sancho Panza, who is the faithful assistant and squire to Don Quixote as he pursues in an unending series of heroic and preposterous adventures the delusional figure of the imagined Dulcinea (Cervantes, 2005). In contrast to Patroclus, Sancho is a humble figure that does not seek to mimic the Don, who is pathetic compared to the mighty Achilles; rather he attempts to modify the more preposterous aspects and attributes of the Don and his audacious behaviour and ambition. Though he is somewhat taken in by the grandeur of the Don's self-proclaimed knighthood and the heroic nature of his quest, he never forgets the purpose and limits of his task, that is, to protect the Don from the many dangers created by his reckless delusions and manic ambition. Unlike Patroclus, he does not put on the armour of Don Quixote nor does he seek his own fame and glory; rather he remains committed to assisting the Don in trying to recover his sanity and to recall the essence of his identity as husband, father, farmer, and member of his community. In spite of the Don's relentless elaboration of his "quest" he gently, persistently, and without scorn seeks to provide the links that might support the rediscovery of the truth of the Don's life.

The value of the *therapon* concept for the therapeutic work with such a depressed, despairing, and resistant patient is the provision of an archetypal structure of containment that recognises the incredible forces operating within both the subject and the therapist and the ways in which the figure of the *therapon* must position himself in order to help the "master" secure his goals without losing herself. Here the term master refers to the necessity of regarding the patient with respect and dignity to fend off the regressive experience of infantilising or demonising him in the countertransference. As has been said, this patient is in the grip of a "primitive agony" (Winnicott, 1974) located at the edge of a breakdown that threatens the collapse of his own sense of value and worth, truly a condition of complete mortification. At the same time he has activated a powerfully delusional element of manic narcissism that enables him to resist recognising the importance of the *therapon* and so continues to cling to the self-generated internal, ideal object used to deny his massive sense of dependency.

Clinical considerations

This chapter has been devoted to offering a new way to understand the problem of chronic and seemingly intractable resistance by establishing a new matrix of theory that emphasises the patient's resistance in and to the treatment to reflect an internal catastrophe that lies behind the seemingly normal surface of what we imagine to be the subject's neurotic experience. Whether the patient is "reluctantly open" or "primarily closed", he is better and more productively understood to be struggling with and against powerful traumatic forces that threaten him at the core of his being and identity.

The modern object relations approach advocated in this chapter (Bion, 1962, 1965, 1970; Fairbairn, 1952; Grotstein, 1979, 2000, 2009; Klein, 1935, 1946; Ogden, 1986, 2002) seeks to discover through the give-and-take of the moment-by-moment unfolding of the transference the cluster of unconscious experience—memories, phantasies, and defences—that hold the meaning, either in represented or unrepresented forms, that will enable the therapist to enter into an empathic and sympathetic connection and temporary, but necessary, unity with the patient. This coming together but remaining separate is one of the key challenges associated with working with the intensely resistant patient. The use of the term "chronic resistance" is better phrased as a "tragic experience" of resistance because it emerges out of the perversity and alienation of the subject's childhood context and is his attempt to fend off the collapse of the self into massive depression and hopelessness.

A patient's resistance is not a "thing-in-itself" (Kant, 1992), something that is unrelated to the psychic and environmental experience of the patient. Rather, it is a nodal point reflecting the action of many forces and experiences that come together as the patient attempts to find an understanding partner that may help him to make sense of his "primitive agonies" (Winnicott, 1974). This patient demands a great investment from the therapist and we must move carefully so that we do not accept the fatalistic premise that he is beyond help and understanding though such a thought must emerge if we are to really understand him. The deadness of sessions that emerges as the patient seeks to enact his problems requires us to develop an ever-greater capacity for symbolic regard and imagination to be able to locate and contain the existential and life-and-death issues at the base of the patient's problems and which emerge as "dramatic derivatives" (Ferro, 2013, p. 4). The following ideas are offered in response to the therapist's natural need of seeking to find tools or tactics that might enable her to reach the patient.

First: Racker (1968) has emphasised that the underlying factors in the therapist that contribute a pathological experience of masochistic involvement with the patient are related to the therapist's "pathological defenses" (p. 144) against her archaic defences and the unresolved conflicts of her internal object relations. Just as the patient defends against a "catastrophe" being repeated, the same holds true for the analyst. The therapist

> finds himself confronted anew with his early crimes. It is often just these childhood conflicts … with their aggression, that led him into this profession in which he tries to repair the objects of the aggression and to overcome or deny his guilt. (p. 145)

The therapist's inability to "get" the patient to improve points to the overreach of the therapist's responsibility and her movement out of the role of the "*therapon*" and into the role of "scapegoat". In such a state she repeats her original aggression towards her parental objects with the intensification of her guilt. The therapist, because of her infantile ideals, represses her awareness of her aggression, and the treatment continues forward in a compromised version where mutual suffering and sacrifice of the therapeutic partnership extend the anti-therapeutic mode of the treatment, that is, the co-creation of an "unanalysable" experience. The emphasis must remain on the examination of the countertransference to determine those factors in the therapist that operate against the discovery of primary points of trauma, guilt, and shame. We have offered the terms "*therapon*" and "scapegoat" to differentiate the role of the therapist in her engagement with the patient.

Second: developing a sense of the true "interpenetration" of the treatment. The patient has been used as the "receptacle" for the pathological projections of his objects (mother, father, family) and he seeks desperately to bring the totality of his experience into the centre of the treatment (Joseph, 1989, chapter 11). It is crucial to recognise that this patient does not have a set of memories and experiences that are available for presentation, understanding, and integration. As we have said, this traumatised patient has developed "zones of non-existence" (Bion, 1970, p. 20) where parts of him ceased to exist as the events of his childhood unfolded. The task confronting the therapist is to understand the ways in which chaos and meaninglessness are often the central meaning of the treatment (Bergstein, 2019).

The demands of attention and containment, the burdens of reverie and imagination continually challenge the therapist to open her mind and relax the judgemental function of her superego. The tragically resistant patient is neither neurotic nor psychotic; he contains a multiplicity of self-states and diagnostic elements. He is depressed, lacks certain psychic structures, has schizoid components but most importantly we must recognise that he seeks to "re-stage," to dramatise the crucial elements of his life that drove him towards the horror of a breakdown experience. Grotstein (2009, p. 224) says that for the most traumatically affected patients the treatment context becomes a "passion play" and the elements of his past reveal that they are still very alive and demanding attention. The therapist is pressured to join the patient in the literal nature of his experience. He has been occupied by these figures and emotions and now the subject seeks to demonstrate, through his enactments what his inner experience actually is. As Davoine and Gaudillière say: "what can't be spoken must be shown" (2004, p. xx). The clinical response is away from confrontation, where a particular reality is asserted and towards an accommodation of the uniqueness of the patient's perspective.

The patient and his problems demand that the therapist descend into the pit of his agony to experience and "to come into contact with and to exist within the patient's zones of non-existence" (Davoine & Gaudillière, 2004, p. 12) that might enable the therapist to weave a social bond, to make a memory where none existed before, and to allow the madness to speak so that the great obstacle at the centre of the self may be encountered. Likewise, it should be noted that because of the extensive splitting of the subject's inner world there is the loss of "ownership" of psychic states (Shengold, 1995). The patient experiences the self acting in destructive or hurtful ways but he makes sure to mask such behaviours from his superego so that no guilt can be felt. In this way, the patient can be very hurtful, perverse, and sadistic to the therapist but encounter no signal of anxiety, guilt, or shame from within his personality. The subject has been hurt, tormented, and tortured and he seeks an opportunity to pay back these attacks, with interest. And indeed, he pushes the frame of the treatment often as far as it will go before he receives the feedback that he has exceeded the boundaries of what can possibly considered to be treatment.

Third: recognising the true nature of the patient's narcissism, that is, it is not merely about feeling important, valuable, or worthy but it exists at the core of the self as a source of energy and power that is different from, though parallel to, libidinal energies and desires. The use of sacrifice and the idea of the god-object are examples of a compensatory register of narcissistic energies of the self where omnipotence and transcendence emerge as a kind of emotional, protective buffer to protect the subject's frail self from a destructive collision with the brute force of external reality.

Fourth: the therapist is faced with the heavy burden of discovering the truth of the patient's life and of being drawn down into the vortex of his experience. We must grieve the limits of what we can do, mourn the passing of many opportunities in order to be able to re-engage the patient as he allows himself to be discovered in the treatment. The core problems of the chronically resistant patient revolve around the earliest attachment and bonding processes (Bowlby, 1958; Spitz, 1965) and are not available to be discussed but rather experienced, endured and brought to life.

Fifth: the struggle with the transference and the battle within us to support our own healthy narcissism as the patient seeks to use us as a scapegoat container for the damage, despair, and trauma of his failed attachment efforts can be monumental. Riviere sees the clinical work with this patient involving the unmasking of the false transference and self-idealisation and bringing together the "true positive and true negative transference" (ibid., p. 152). She warns of the lurking complexity of this patient:

> A false and treacherous transference ... is such a blow to our narcissism, and so poisons and paralyses our instrument for good (our understanding of the patient's unconscious mind), that it tends to rouse strong depressive anxieties in ourselves. So the patient's falseness often enough meets with denial by us and remains unseen and unanalyzed by us too. (Riviere, 1991, p. 153)

Sixth: the patient's battle with the elements at the core of the mind–self that seek life and those that seek death need to be kept in mind. The pain of loss, the feelings of isolation and alienation can be seen to drive the subject towards psychosomatic (beta) conditions. With this tragically resistant patient the presence of bodily states and conditions is often the clearest form of communication possible.

Likewise, the subject's retreat into drug and alcohol use/abuse is another sign of the overwhelming intensity of the traumatic pain and the threat he feels as the treatment deepens and moves ever closer to the breakdown element that is lurking at the core of the self. Separation from, and the mourning of, the infantile attachment to the primary object becomes a looming catastrophe that must be approached with the utmost care and respect.

Seventh: is the patient treatable? This question emerges when the therapist, after many years, asks herself if the therapy can possibly emerge as a vital and life-giving form of understanding, support, and transformation. The severe states of traumatic experience place the subject in the double bind of seeking desperately to escape from the crypt of his tormenting but failed attachment and, similarly, of constructing the treatment as an endless battle against the dangers of separation and individuation. The patient has suffered and bears the scars that limit growth and development but in no way excludes it. The ideas, theories, and attitudes in this chapter and book seek to support the therapist as she moves, slowly and by degrees, into the transitional realm between the subject's frozen self and contact with the alive but tentative components that, if understood and developed in a mutual and interpenetrating experience, can yield the rewards of growth and development. As Freud advised in "Mourning and melancholia" (1917e) the patient must be helped to find and recognise his desire to remain trapped in the infantile but omnipotent world of the child. The work of the treatment, both in the depressive position and in the oedipal context, is to help the patient find the courage to face his dreadful task of, as Ogden (2002) states: "to grieve the loss of the object, one must first kill it, that is, one must do the psychological work of allowing the object to be irrevocably dead, both in one's own mind and in the external world" (p. 779). In this way we enable the patient, where possible, to move from the object as "ghost" to the object as a nurturing "ancestor" and thereby be open to the discovery of new objects (Loewald, 1980, p. 249).

CHAPTER TWO

The scapegoat sacrifice: Repeat or reprieve?

Karen Fraley

It is that we are never so defenceless against suffering as when we love, never so helplessly unhappy as when we have lost our loved object or its love.

—Freud, 1930a, p. 82

The choice that matters to the psycho-analyst is one that lies between procedures designed to evade frustration and those designed to modify it. That is the critical decision.

—Bion, 1962, p. 29, original emphasis

Expanding the capacity to suffer emotional pain is one of the main tasks of therapy (Bion 1962; Symington 2007a). Paying close attention to defences against frustration and anxiety, the therapist picks up the signs of each patient's resistances and the resounding cues in the therapist's self against the communication of emotional pain and the experiencing of it. Patients and therapists alike seek to avoid emotional pain through casting blame against others and against the self. At the same time, each one seeks an ideal object to transform suffering thereby restoring an ideal world, the world as we feel it should be.

Bion (1962) gives us the concepts of positive and negative links to help us distinguish between defensive mental activities intending to avoid frustration and emotional pain, and mental activities designed to accept and modify painful emotional experiences. Bion proposed three primary emotional links: K for knowledge and wanting-to-know; L for love and the desire for connection with the other; and H for hate, or autonomy, separateness, and the courage to stand alone. He conceived of positive links as affective couplings forming the connective tissue of the internal world, linking emotional experiences in the body with the conscious, thinking mind. Through the linking process experiences are rendered into a form suitable for remembering and further thinking. These thoughts then require a thinker to make meaning of them. Psychic work consisting of generative, integrative, and synthesising activities enrich the self (Bion, 1962), creating new internal objects and mourning the loss of others. Pleasurable experiences as well as painful ones, once linked, can be thought about in a way that strengthens and grows the self (Symington, 2017), increasing the capacity to accept and tolerate the realities of life. This internal connectivity builds the psychic structure necessary for acknowledgement of the internal world, separate and distinct from the external, and at the same time, connected and in flux, each enriching the other.

While positive linking functions activate an arborescence of the mind in rooting, branching, and growing, coextensive negative linking functions protect the mind from experiencing intolerably painful emotions. These negative linking activities—identified by Bion (1962) as negative K or wanting-to-not-know, negative L or indifference and not caring, and negative H or denial of separateness from the loved other—throw the engine of the mind into reverse, cancelling out experience to protect a fragile self and exerting powerful controls over the object relation. Negative linking activities represent tormenting and painful reactions to traumatic experiences, resulting in chaotic internal states, actively intending to destroy conscious awareness and thinking. Incapacitating the symbolic functions of the mind, negative linking functions denude synthesising processes, impairing the ego's capacities to accept the realities of life and to create new object relations.

Despite the therapist's best efforts to reach the painful sufferings of a patient the negative linking activities sabotage the therapeutic process, often by casting blame on others, or the self, for feelings of helplessness and despair. I suggest one form of negative linking takes place through a scapegoating of the self, a type of sacrifice effectively cancelling out positive linking functions. The scapegoat sacrifice enacts negative link functions, erasing, denying, and obliterating subjective experience, narrative, and history, avoiding the agonising pain of frustrations, injuries, and deficits in the self. The sacrifice instantiates an identification with a god-like object (as Charles Ashbach has termed this form of an ideal object) through violently attacking the truth-seeking capacities of the mind. Fusion with the ideal object seems, in fantasy, to be possible once the eradication of the scapegoated part of the self takes place.

Elusive and tricky, the scapegoat identifications move between the twin poles of an ideal self in relation to an ideal object, and an excoriated, banished, scapegoat part of the self. In the therapy relationship, unconscious scapegoat identifications can seamlessly shift between the patient or the therapist as the scapegoat. In moments when the patient blames the therapist for her limited effectiveness in handling the treatment, unable to erase and undo the patient's agony, and unable to revive the lost, loved object, the patient may see the therapist as the scapegoat. In other moments, the therapist may scapegoat the patient, casting blame for the failed treatment onto the patient's inability to "take in" the good object provided by the therapist. The mercurial scapegoat dynamic can take hold of the therapy process, immobilising the developing functions of the ego, attacking links (Bion, 1962) between affect, memories, and thought, stopping time, and emptying the aliveness of the therapy field.

The patients I am thinking of often come to therapy full of optimism, yet soon present a narrative of self-blame, and dreadful disappointments, with a distinct lack of affective contact. Highly sensitive, and at the same time cut off from his emotions, the patient believes something catastrophic will occur if he reveals his true emotions, as if emotions carry omnipotent power.

Negative linking activities cut off the communication of internal emotional experiences from contact with others, and from opportunities to test internal world realities against the realities of the external world. The sequestered internal world assumes the conviction that the self is to blame for all failures and tasked with repairing all injuries. Mired in an all-or-nothing world, thinking processes bog down, constricting the flow of the exchange within the therapy relationship.

Marking a sharp edge between the emotional self and the thinking mind, maintained at any cost, promotes a sensitivity to an interpretation from a different point of view, aggravating the already painful schism. When touched by the therapist, deep currents of shame can flood the patient further, constricting the dialogue and causing a breach in the therapeutic alliance. Comments aimed towards opening up space to think and feel, fall flat, disappearing into a void. Time and again, the therapist might feel shut out and dismissed, as if forced to sacrifice therapeutic functions and capacities.

Therapists hear of endless recriminations against the self, and the cruel injustices of others but find no way to reach the injured, frightened, and traumatised self in the background, underneath a shroud of shame and guilt. It is as if a key part of the self has been cast away in order to save an essential tie to the lost loved object, and the hope of staying alive depends on maintaining this tie. The scapegoated self substitutes for someone felt to be liable for the emotional catastrophe threatening the existence of the self. The patient attempts to locate and overpower the cause of his suffering, and at the same time, communicates his hope to end his suffering, once and for all. The scapegoat identification points to the existence of a catastrophic event, defends against the impact of it, and communicates the hope for salvation through devotions to an ideal object.

I hope to illustrate these ideas in the clinical setting with the following vignettes from long-term, once-a-week psychotherapies of men and women patients. The details are disguised and may or may not be a composite case. Illustrations showing the exchanges in the sessions are followed by discussions of my thoughts and elaborations after the sessions. The vignettes focus on the early phase of treatment where the difficulties of establishing contact with the patient point to disruptions and turmoil in relationship with the primary maternal object (this could be mother, father, or a combination). Similarly, the process of establishing and forming a therapeutic relationship followed the pattern of impoverished and disjointed surfaces.

Case description

The patient, whom I have named Vickie, unmarried and childless, seemed to be a twenty-year-old woman in the body of a fifty-year-old. When I first met Vickie, I noticed a tension in her face and body, as if she was intent on holding herself together. She wore a tight black skirt with a button-up shirt, her brown hair pulled back tightly and smoothly and held by a ribbon matching the bright blue of her painted fingernails and toes, as if put together perfectly in a child-like way, untouched by age. Her body movements appeared angular and tense. Sitting on the couch she seemed not to want to touch anything, as if curled up inside, trying not to take up too much room. With a slight stutter she managed to overcome each time her throat would catch, Vickie found few words to fit her experience.

Competent in her profession, and well-established financially, and with years of therapy behind her, Vickie continued to feel a profound unease within herself.

She remembered very little of her childhood, saying long periods of time were lost to her. Terribly ill with lupus, her mother was often away from home receiving treatment at the hospital. Her father was estranged, saying he was at work, and coming home only when her mother needed to go to the hospital. In the early phase of treatment Vickie tended to focus exclusively on her relationship with her mother. When home and recovering, her mother would look as if she was well, but would say she felt sick, staying in bed for days at a time, darkening her room to keep the sun out and closing the door as a sign that she wanted to be left alone. Vickie remembered returning home from school, doing the housework and then sequestering herself in her room, quiet and alone. As Vickie described this scene, I felt an electrified tension in the room, as if a high tensile line of expectation and dependency stretched to the breaking point in the silent space between Vickie and her mother, and now between us.

As an adult, Vickie described often waking up with a jolt of anxiety, instantly worried and immediately judging herself as worthless. Whenever she excelled at work, she immediately felt others disliked her. A compulsion to do what others thought she should do, to please them and help them, even to rescue them, motivated her daily actions. At work she was the person everyone went to for help and she noticed that she compulsively accepted this role without question as if forced to deliver what everyone needs. She would like to change jobs but has no idea what she would be qualified to do, as if she had no skills or experience to support her ambitions.

Continuing, Vickie reported she talks to her mother every day, and that yesterday mother had called with a computer problem. Vickie walked her through the solutions to the problem, being a computer tech, but her mother said that didn't work. Completely rejecting Vickie's suggestions, she demanded that Vickie come over and fix it for her. Vickie had a meeting and could not go, then felt panicky and guilty. She had to fix it for her mother. She always did that. If she didn't, she'd abandon her mother, who would then be angry with her. She knew her mother was angry when she called her back the next morning and disdainfully said she had fixed it herself. She had called the computer company and they had helped her. Feeling rebuked and punished, cut out by her mother, Vickie's despair and terror set in.

Would her mother ever talk to her again? When she was a child her mother would cut out, not speaking, and refusing to come out of her room for days at a time. Then suddenly she'd start talking again without warning or apology, as if nothing had happened. The rule was that no one was to say anything about "cutting out". That would upset her mother and she'd withdraw again. Vickie felt pressured to go along with her mother to avoid any conflict, and, in turn, Vickie remained silent, cutting out the memory of what had happened, and feeling used and battered inside.

Vickie paused and shifted her position on the couch, looking towards the window, tensing herself, as she described her dream to start her own weaving business, raising sheep, collecting and dyeing the wool, managing and nurturing the animals, establishing a seamless cycle of renewal from animal to woven product, and joining up with other weavers, a circle of women she could rely on. Safe and secure in an interdependent system, the sheep depending on her as she depended on them, her eyes brimmed with tears and her voice faltered as she described her hope for relief from the pressures of taking care of others.

I felt stunned by Vickie's dream to live inside an interdependent eco-system cancelling out the dangers and benefits of a genuine, depressive position dependency. I thought of sheep as submissive with very few defences, and easily frightened. Responding to her, I comment that she wishes for a place of her own where she can take care of her needs by herself.

Vickie described her chronic feelings of loneliness, often feeling she's on an island, solo. Everyone else is interacting, and having a good time, but she is alone. Talking with her mother, she described feeling splintered inside, as if tiny needle-sharp pieces of her fell away and disappeared. During these times she focused on work, going about her job in a robotic way, keeping herself in motion, not knowing where she was and feeling she did not matter to anyone. Questioning her right to exist, Vickie doubted that anything she wanted or felt mattered, and this became a theme through the therapy. I noted to myself that "matter" comes from the root word "mater", meaning "mother" (Online Etymology Dictionary). The basis of the source of aliveness insider her appeared to be fractured, ruptured, and evaporated.

Listening to Vickie, I remembered the scene in a sci-fi story I had read long ago about two robots from the future trying to kill each other as their spaceship spins out of control. One robot takes a direct hit from the other, but instead of instantly collapsing, he explodes into tiny, crystallised fragments each disparate and distinct, flinging away in all directions, flooding the spaceship. Suddenly and magically, the crystallised splinters reverse their movement, hurling back towards each other, effortlessly reassembling the robot back into his original form. He stands whole and triumphant in his invulnerability, as if gaining power through this destruction.

As other patients with a history of trauma have described, once splintered, Vickie longed for an immediate and magical reassembly. On the weekends, when her anxiety hit her like a tornado, she has no idea what this is about, or where it comes from. The whole experience feels alien to her, as if her fear does not come from inside her or take place in her body. Convinced there is nothing she can do, she isolates herself, refusing to eat or speak, until gradually she reconstitutes herself.

I found myself becoming tired, disoriented, and lost, my thoughts swirling into a vortex of phantasmagorical splinters. Suffused with too much, my mind began to sink into passivity, effectively "cutting out". Vickie seemed to fill the room with her despair and her splintered state of mind. Struggling to revive my thinking and hold my place I said, "When the tornado hits and you feel splintered, there is no one to turn to."

In a contemptuous, cold tone Vickie responded, "If you need someone, and say anything about what you need from them, you get cut, like the animal in a trap gnawing off its paw to save itself." I felt the sting of her coldness and the cruelty she expressed for her lack of maternal care. The only way to go on was to "cut out" her experiences, gnawing off a part of herself and moving on. I thought she showed me, as well, her reaction to my cutting out. It was clear that Vickie felt she was not to need anything or express anger or frustration to her mother. In her mind one cut deserves another and that is a solution to her pain.

I wondered what was going on inside of Vickie when her mother cut her out. What kinds of decisions and assumptions was she making about how the world works and how people treat each other? What parts of her was she cutting out?

Vickie described carrying her mother, as if she carried a dead weight on her back. She felt responsible for fixing her mother. If she cut out her mother, she could not survive. Her only hope was to be the loving daughter she was supposed to be, becoming a mother to her mother, making everything right, and then she would get what she desperately needed. It was her fault if that did not happen.

Responding to her experience of being cut out, I said "Something terrible took place inside you when you felt cut off from your mother. You thought you were to blame, and this helped you to continue on, but you carry the weight of this blame on your back."

She responded saying she always felt something was wrong with her and it is her fault. No matter what she does for others she always feels guilty. She finished by saying she wants me to figure out what is wrong inside her and to fix it, like a computer technician repairing a faulty computer.

Suddenly gripped by a feeling of dread, I felt a tremendous responsibility for her, and for the phantasy that I would cut into her and "fix" her without her knowing what was wrong. Perhaps she will cut me out and carry on with her solution to "fix" herself and "cut out" her needs, if I do not carry her on my back.

Discussion

Vickie began the session signalling her despair and feelings of abandonment in response to a needy mother, who she felt used and neglected her. She experienced her empty-breast mother as a cruel mother, withholding her nourishing loving care, remaining closed off and cut out. I imagined Vickie as an infant, crying and hungry, without a good breast presenting itself for her to attack and take in. Instead, Vickie felt she must fill her mother up, inflate her breast before she could take anything for herself. An empty, greedy mother figure pervaded her internal world, intensifying her desire to be nursed and carried by a good maternal object.

In Vickie's view, her mother's needs cut into her needs. Cut off from her mother, and from her herself, she can only say "I don't matter", cancelling out the painful emptiness that is too much to bear. Cut off from herself, her inner world ruptures into fragments, flying every which way. Cutting links between herself and her mother, and her experiences, emotions, and needs, her world becomes persecutory, leaving her feeling fragmented. Immobilised, she waited out the internal catastrophe, relying on a magical restoration like the robot in the science fiction story.

A robotic killing machine, the robot appears human, but his metallic exoskeleton has supernatural powers. When attacked, he explodes into crystallised bits without the pain of bleeding and torn flesh. In a matter of seconds, the robotic body magically reconstitutes itself. Without bearing any traces of the violent trauma he has just endured, the robot carries on unperturbed. Vickie imagines a magical regeneration of herself, mechanically, without feeling, and single-handedly, as if she could rebirth herself after suffering a death blow, an unfathomable narcissistic injury. No mourning is required. The rebirth is an immaculate birth, without a gestation period, or labour pains, denying the experience of destruction as if it had never occurred.

Vickie's disintegration reminds me of the myth of the Egyptian goddess Isis, a primitive maternal figure. When Set, a sibling god, killed Osiris, the husband of Isis, by closing him in a box and flinging him into the River Nile, Isis retrieved the body, and hiding it in a swamp, preserved it until she could arrange a full burial with the required mourning period. But Set goes hunting that night and finding the coffin, becomes enraged. He then chops Osiris' body into pieces, dismembering him and flinging the pieces throughout Egypt, ensuring that Isis can never find them. Set represents chaos and murder, a figure attacking links and the integration brought about through mourning. Isis and her sister scour the world to retrieve the scattered pieces of Osiris. Piece by piece Isis reassembled Osiris and breathed life into him. When only one piece was missing, his penis, Isis, with another god's help, fashioned a golden penis and attached it to Osiris' body, and then conceived a child with him. The myth of Isis and Osiris represents the cycle of death, mourning, search, recovery, and rebirth (Neumann, 1954). In reassembling Osiris, she re-members him. Through her remembering, she creates new life, and new objects through the linking processes of mourning.

The robot figure is devoid of the capacity to mourn, and to love, and has no experience of human frailty and helplessness. He survives, but does not learn or develop, and is doomed to endlessly repeat the same behaviour. Vickie suffers the continued pattern of fixing the other at the expense of herself (Riviere, 1936), unable to recognise herself as she is, holding on instead to an image of herself before the loss, untainted by experience. For Vickie, and other patients with this type of trauma, gathering the splintered pieces of her experiences, holding them, and engaging in the work of mourning, seemed like plunging into a deep despair she could not recover from. Without a good enough containing object inside she cannot hold herself while she re-members the child who lost out (Green, 1986), taking courage to bear the feelings long enough to make meaning of them.

Vickie's interest in becoming a weaver and her wish to join a fold of people bound to a common way of life could potentially signal a turn towards the depressive position, a movement towards suffering the painful ebbing and flowing of the cycle of life. Yet I sensed that Vickie wished to weave a cocoon or a womb to hold her in a smooth and seamless body within an ideal maternal object, as if to give birth to herself. This wish expressed the hope for an identification with an ideal mother, who could be used without damage, or fear of retribution, and continually renewed, without separation or sorrow. This is a common theme for those patients who have experienced maternal neglect. In her deep hunger for contact Vickie mobilised her mind to dream up a solution to her pain, and this dream structured her hope of surviving and becoming alive in herself.

Forced to carry the dead weight of her mother, who, in her mind was always on her back, she felt persecuted and responsible for the deadness of her contact with her mother. Is she alive and vital inside herself, or essentially miscarried or aborted? Vickie did not know who or what she was guilty for, or the crime she needed to atone for.

Vickie alerted me to the problem of her carrying me, as if my interpretations and observations would land on her, pushing something into her in just the way she felt her intrusive, needy mother did. If I gather the splintered bits of her and try to recognise her, and put the pieces together, will she feel forced to carry my interpretations? If I fail to "fix" her, will she feel re-injured? I wondered how much of *her* she actually feels is her. How much of her is in the room with me?

Vickie wished to omnipotently "fix" her mother by being the perfect daughter. The word "fix" has many meanings. I would like to mention a few of them here.

To "fix" means to stabilise, to attach, to hold steady, as in "fixing her eyes upon an object"; to assign, as in "fixing blame"; to repair, to cure, and to "fix" an animal is to castrate or spay it (Merriam Webster Dictionary).

The Latin root of the word means to "thrust in; pierce through, transfix" (Online Etymology Dictionary). "Transfixing" references nailing down, as in nailed to a cross in a crucifixion. At the same time, "fixing" is used to "restore, or attach" an object. The word contains definitions of both "fixing in place" and "restoring and repairing". We see here the close connection between assigning blame in order to locate the cause of failures and problems, and the wish for repair, transformation, and the hope of restoring a connection to an undamaged object.

To "fix" also refers to controlling the outcome, or the winner, of a game or contest. Before the contest starts, fixing arbitrarily determines the victor, according to a preconceived plan, and not as the outcome of the process or contest. Fixing the therapy process according to one's own world view, matching the ideal object, and affirming a preconceived belief, is also possible. This fixing of her internal world created an impasse in the therapy, blocking the emergence of her split-off experiences into the warmth of the therapy relationship. Vickie wanted my help to cut out her damaged self, fixing her and also keeping her experiences banished beyond reach of the weaving and containing process between us, preventing the necessary acknowledgement of her emotional truths. Tragically, the very strategy she uses to fix herself prevents her from creating a different outcome. Just as the robot in outer space was preprogramed to fix himself, preventing development through the process of learning, or giving birth to the self through the attention of a containing other, Vickie attempted to fix the outcome of the therapy, fixing me in a role assigned by her, as a computer technician, according to her preconceived plan.

"Fixing" her mother became her fixation, preoccupying her mind, in order to steady her world, a form of "private religion" (Freud, 1907, p. 119), serving to hold her genuine self in a cocoon, in abeyance until she could find a reliable source of life. She must continue to "fix" her mother, cutting out the damage and erasing the terrible truth that she never truly *had* her mother or existed in her mother's mind. For this reason, she could never leave her mother or separate from her to find herself.

Freud's concept of a "fixed idea" (Freud, 1920g, p. 13) seems applicable here. Defined as a preoccupation of the mind believed to be firmly resistant to any attempt to modify it, such as a fixation, the delusion is held firmly in place denying both internal and external reality. Vickie believed that she could repair her mother to become the mother she needed, effectively erasing her trauma, rage, and terror. At the same time, this fixed idea protects her idealisation of her mother, affirming her as a good mother, who only needs a good daughter. This idealisation became crucial to Vickie's emotional survival. Vickie determined to be the good daughter, thereby creating the good mother, cutting out the certainty that she felt she had destroyed her good mother with her aggressive and needy demands (Riviere, 1936). Fixing her mother fixes her as an alive, hopeful, and loving person, connected to a capable and loving mother. To do this she must cleave her "bad daughter" part away, breaching the gap for her "good daughter" self to affix to her "good mother". If she fails to fix her mother, then the source of the failure resides in her. She is to blame. Here is the scapegoat identification, as if to say: "Through my sacrifice I revivify my dead mother and prove my love for her. Failing that I am the reason for her despair, and I must atone for my failure by repeatedly sacrificing myself."

The scapegoat, a surrogate sacrificial victim (Girard, 1986), initially blameless, takes the blame to protect an attachment to a needed and feared primary other. In tasking herself to fix her mother, she turns the hatred she felt coming from her mother against herself, cutting out the hungry and helpless infant-self, desperately in need of a containing mother. The cutting out is an act of revenge meted out against herself, through the negative H link. The scapegoat sacrifice assumes an emotional quid pro quo under the rubric of the law of talion, a primitive retributive form of justice in which the crime demands an equally destructive punishment such as "an eye for an eye or a tooth for a tooth". The law of talion establishes an omnipotent psychic structure in a splintered, ravaged internal world.

Hollowed out so that no traces of her subjectivity remain, the scapegoated self absorbs the painful blame assigned to it by the scapegoating ego-ideal. The scapegoat victim takes the role of a substitute (Girard, 1986) carrying the burden of guilt for the limitations and failures of others. Yet the scapegoat participates in carrying the blame in order to reach a higher level of identification with the god-object. The banishment of the scapegoated self purifies and cleanses the world, as if, once the bad object is cleared away, the ideal object will automatically appear, instantly righting all wrongs.

Through the scapegoat identification, one part of the self, a lofty ideal aspect, exploits the dependent part of the self, remaining indifferent (negative L) to its plight (Stoller, 1975). The subjective integrity of the victim is sadistically ignored, through the negative H link, destroying the structures and realities of the internal world of the subject. Reversing the victim–victimiser roles, what was passively and helplessly experienced becomes magically converted into an action of power and control.

Case description

After one year of therapy, Vickie arrived for her session agitated and upset. She had witnessed an accident on the highway. A deer had suddenly charged across the road into the middle of traffic. Cars swerved, trying not to hit each other. Then she saw the corpse of the deer, mangled and broken, its spilled blood seeping into the pavement. Everyone got out of their car to look. They love seeing blood and guts. There was nothing she could do.

She wanted to get away as fast as possible but had to wait, crawling along the highway with everyone else.

Discussion

I thought of the blood spilled on her internal highway, blocking traffic, immobilising her world, and potentially alerting me to a sacrificial bloodletting. Perhaps the spilled blood relates to the violent attack she felt when her mother failed to attend and care for her. Or perhaps the blood communicates the blood link with her mother, a cruel link, but mesmerising and preserved in a repetitive sacrificial ritual.

Blood signifies death and irreparable injury, indicating a painful wound that still bleeds, like a wound that cannot heal. Could her annoyance with stopping to see the blood and guts have to do with the therapy process, stopping to see the injuries and losses in her, rather than speed past them?

Perhaps the sacrificial blood bridges the gap inside Vickie's world between the desire for contact and the pain of realising the absence of the very contact she expected to find with her mother and now with me. In addition, blood represents birth and new life, linked to her feminine self that bleeds each month. The blood on the highway, an external event, might also signify the potential birth of a new awareness, born of her experience.

The word psychotherapist comes from the ancient Greek word "therapeutikos" derived from "therapeutein" meaning "to cure, treat medically, primarily 'do service, take care of, provide for', and is related to 'therapon', meaning attendant" (Online Etymology Dictionary). Nagy (1979), a classics professor specialising in the tales of Homer, finds the word "*therapon*" in the *Iliad* and the *Odyssey*, and makes the point that in Ancient Greek literature the *therapon* is the "alter-ego" (p. 292), or we could say the double, of the warrior he attends. The *therapon* becomes identified with the warrior, "attending" (Nagy, 1979, p. 292) to his state of mind, caring for his armour, his horses, his emotional and physical needs, and readying him for battle.

While the practice of psychotherapy is not the same as a military battle, Davoine (2016) maintains that "psychic survival requires the presence of a 'therapon', to use Homer's term, an attendant with whom it is vital to speak. Achilles had Patroclus, and Don Quixote had Sancho Panza" (p. xiv). The *therapon* keeps the space to speak about the dangers of the ideal object and the desires for the good object.

Noting that the term *therapon* often refers to a relationship between two men, I asked how the *therapon* relationship might be different between women. What happens when two women work together in the battle for the psychological survival of one? How might this relationship differ from that between two men?

I think the term "mid-wife" might be one way women have traditionally engaged the role of the *therapon*. The midwife "attends" to the woman in childbirth, staying with her, caring for her, taking responsibility for her survival while the woman "labours" to give birth. The midwife cannot labour for the woman, only stay with her, encourage her, attend her suffering in giving birth, and assuring her survival. Chasseguet-Smirgel (1985) references the metaphor of analysis as a new birth, stating that in this view "[a]nalysis is, here, literally speaking, a maieutic" (p. 116), and the root of this word "maieutic" means "to acts as a midwife" (Online Etymological Dictionary).

Applying the term *therapon* to my work, I suggest the therapist attends to the suffering of the patient, attempting to move the suffering from a banished, deadened state to an active, generative suffering, holding the courage necessary for the patient to represent the insufferable, giving birth to new aspects of the self and new internal objects. Just as Isis created a birth from her remembering of Osiris, I wonder if Vickie could give birth to herself through the active re-membering and re-working of her trauma in the psychotherapy process.

Case description

In a subsequent session Vickie reported attending a yoga class. When the instructor moved to a backward stretch pose, requiring her to open her chest and reach behind her, electrifying terror shot through her body. She was sure she would fall back and crash her head. She couldn't breathe, she felt her spine would break and splinter into bits right in her middle, leaving her forever broken. Unable to speak, she stopped and tried to get her breath. No one said anything. She wanted to cry but told herself she must *not* cry, there where everyone could *see* her. She imagined the splinters were stuck and festering inside her. She had no idea what was going on or why she was feeling this way, no link to her body or emotions. She fled the yoga class not knowing what to do with herself, she just knew she had to get out of the room and away from people. She felt sure this fear and shame had to do with talking so much about her mother in the therapy.

I thought of her crashing backwards, and the deer crashing into the truck on the highway. Did she feel I was crashing into her, forcing her to talk about her mother, increasing her suffering rather than alleviating it? I realised she was signalling the intensity of her suffering, a pain she experienced beyond her capacity to feel and think. Picturing her waiting for her mother, somewhere in the house yet invisible, I imagined a child with an emotional world of splintered bits, unable to weave them together, her containing threads splintered.

She described the fear of having something wrong inside her, and memories of not being able to breathe, her throat tight and clogged, as if strangled by something inside her. When I said to her these very painful experiences were being remembered in her body, which she feared she could not survive, she paused for a few minutes. Continuing, she said that as a child she had chronic backache. It felt like her back was breaking and she would often come home from school early because the pain got so bad. Her mother didn't believe her and thought she was just trying to get out of going to school. The school nurse was sympathetic but didn't do much to help her. I thought of this as a transference statement referring to me as another caring professional who doesn't do much to help her. The doctor didn't know what to make of it and finally, after months of this, she was diagnosed with H. pylori, a stomach parasite. Once treated she felt better but always had the sense that something parasitic was inside her, breaking her down and feeding on her.

I imagined what it might be like for her to tolerate the splintering pain inside her, and to allow her mind to attend to that pain, and what this might mean for her. If she could manage this, she would be mothering herself, and perhaps could stay in contact with herself. Mothering seemed equated with contacting the damaged part of her, triggering a gut-wrenching anguish in her, and a deep sadness that she feels she must cut out, rather than bear. Attempting to hold this space in myself I fought the pressure of my guilt for having caused her suffering, and the temptation to join her belief that the therapy was a source of her pain, rather than a means to experience and potentially to integrate the pain she carried inside.

Suddenly, Vickie remembered a dream from childhood, saying:

I am high up in the tree behind our house. I climb up a big thick rope, easily, and I climb so far up I know my mother can't find me. I stay there and wait for her to come looking for me. I feel excited waiting for her and then watching her frantically looking for me. I don't say anything. She comes to the bottom of the tree but does not look up. Watching her I want to scream at her, but I stop myself and stay still. As I watch her, I am overjoyed. Suddenly, she walks away. Then everything gets dark and I can't see. The rope is cut, dangling there, and I *can't* climb down. I am too far UP. I am stuck and terrified. The tree starts to shake and tremble, falling apart, and splintering. I am going to fall. Everything will come crashing down. Then I wake up.

Vickie describes feeling the dream as a concrete thing inside her, immutable, wordless, and frightening. At first, she feels excited by her desire for her mother, enlivened and powerful. She is above her mother, looking down, watching her without her mother knowing, tremendously excited. Then seeing her mother turn away, terror strikes like lightning, paralysing her. She watches her mother walk away, as if she doesn't care, as if she lives in a different room or universe, and there is no rope to connect them. Her mother is on the ground, and she is stuck, banished to the top of the tree as if punished for the badness inside her. Locked up and locked out, she can't get back down into herself. Not being seen, she does not exist, now evaporated and invisible. Screaming would validate her existence, but some part of her forbids this act of autonomy and self-recognition. She must not be seen to be taking anything for herself, even if the thing she is taking is revenge.

In response to Vickie's dream, I said: "You felt unwanted, unloved, and you could not show this. You desperately needed your mother, yet thought you must stay hidden, with the hope that she would find you, but she did not." Her eyes blazed at me, and she was silent. She looked away and everything stopped. I felt plunged into darkness, not able to see. She remained silent for several long minutes. Now I am the target of her rage. I am stuck up in the tree and she is walking away, furious and impermeable to my presence. Cold and indifferent to her needs she distances herself from her feelings of shame and vulnerability.

In this way, needs are put into her by others and do not well up from within her. Others are to blame for her needs, painful and frightening as they are. This description of the characteristics of a traumatised state sounded familiar, an experience expressed by other patients in different ways, along with the survival strategy to recover the self through distancing from overwhelming experiences. Staying in this moment to find my thoughts took tremendous effort as my mind filled with many thoughts at once. The silence widened and beginning to feel disoriented and lost, I said to her: "Something happened just now between us."

In an angry, flat tone, she says: "I don't know. I am thinking of other things. Things I have to get at the grocery store on the way home." I think to myself, she is holding the knife in her hand now.

I say: "In the dream you want to scream but tell yourself to stay silent."

She says: "What I feel doesn't matter. I have to be perfect to be loved. If something goes wrong, it's my fault." Holding the cut rope, dangling between us, Vickie leaves me down below with no connection to her. It's a zone of emptiness, controlled by her, and she remains behind the line of contact. Highly invested in her identification with the ideal, she maintains a dissociated zone of no-contact, at the cost of her authentic self. In the dream she is terrified, and yet, high in her tree, she maintains a powerful position near the heavens, but without roots or ties to the object to bring her back down.

I say: "I think in this moment I am the mother who does not see you, does not find you when you most need her."

She says: "It is safe up here. If you see me, everything will burst into splinters again." Noting the tension between us I said: "Remaining up in the tree keeps you safe from the danger of needing others, yet out of reach, and unable to get the connection you need to reach the ground." I felt the bind she was in: to emerge from her retreat threatens her lifeline connected to an ideal mother. If she descends into herself, connecting to her actual object mother, she suffers the loss of the ideal mother she had conjured up inside, facing the pain she actually experienced.

She said: "Yes I want to come down. I want to feel myself, really be myself. I think if I come down and face you, if I look into your eyes, I will see the contempt and rage you have for me. Then I must be guilty. If I stay up in the tree, I feel fine, everything is smooth and effortless."

I think she wants me to know what she is feeling, without having to spell it out, keeping a smooth connection with no glitches or gaps. In this way, she lets me carry her rage and contempt, her painful reactions to feeling cut out, until she can claim positive links to these emotional states in herself. Cutting out the failure in connection, she also cuts through to attempt to find and attain the object she needs. I think of the rope in her dream as an umbilical cord and coming down from the tree as a representation of the voyage down the birth canal to a new and frightening world of objects where Vickie would be responsible for breathing life into herself.

Discussion

Vickie's experience, in the yoga class, of her vulnerable body, liable to rupture into unidentifiable bits, sent shockwaves through her. Unable to stabilise herself through positive linking functions, and attacking the links to her dependent self, the splintered parts of her threaten to amass, proliferating and consuming her internal world.

Split-off and unrepresented emotional pain in the form of beta elements (Bion, 1962) become the key ingredients of "anxiety, dread, and omnipotent thinking" (Symington, 2017). Outside the dimensions of reality testing, in a dream-like state and beyond the reach of conscious awareness and of a relating other, beta element ingredients cook in the pot on the backburner, slowly transformed by the heat of unconscious phantasies. The witches in Shakespeare's play *Macbeth*, having filled their cauldron with various bizarre bits and fragments, sing while they stir the pot and conjure up the future: "Double, double, toil and trouble, Fire burn, and cauldron bubble" (*Macbeth*, 4.1.10–11); so Vickie stirs the pot inside her, filled with unknown and unthought ingredients. Intended for preservation in their original form, split-off beta elements do not remain static or frozen in time. Rather unconscious processes work these elements into elaborated belief systems, expectations, and idealisations, embodied in an unconscious part of the mind, as if somatically inscribed.

The scapegoat identification delivers control and a false empowerment, fueling Vickie's hope to remain untouched by her emotions. But suddenly in the yoga class, the scapegoated parts threaten to return, persecuting her, and perhaps retaliating against her. Terrified, she fears her shameful deficiencies prove her unfit for contact with others and she must flee.

Without a sufficient, internal container to hold her, psychic pain remains intolerable, unrepresented, and unthinkable. Unable to effectively internalise a containing maternal figure, she remains tied to her deficient maternal object. Protesting the injustice of not having enough, she destroys the distinctions between self and other, fragmenting both. Who is abandoning her in the tree? By whom is she trapped? Who is safe and who is angry? It's impossible to tell. Filled with frustration, unable to come out and unable to sustain herself within, she remains trapped. Silently screaming, her violent emotions attack the maternal container, creating a monstrous mother attacking her links, destroying her connection and preventing her descent from the safety of the identification with her ideal object.

The dream shows Vickie's revenge, attacking her mother from her perch in the tree, safe from her mother's retaliation. In her furious, destructive rage, a tormenting revenge is continuously replayed in her mind, a sadistic triumph over her damaged, maternal object, and her masochistic nursing of her wound (Steiner, 1993). It is as if she is saying: "I am showing you how much you hurt me by keeping you out, and at the same time I am blaming you for your betrayal of me. And you can't do anything about it." In these cases, as Steiner (1993) says, "Revenge is neither openly enacted nor given up" (p. 75). Now in control of the attack, instead of the helpless victim, she perpetrates revenge on herself and her objects at the same time.

In the dream, the threshold of transitional space (Winnicott, 1951) between self and other, or mother and child, is turned into a battleground, a "zone of non-existence" as Davoine and Gaudillière (2004, p. 12) write, rather than a transitional mix-up of self and other, where the self can be discovered. The establishment of transitional space depends on the inherent trust of the mother–child bond. The mother on the other side of the space must be trustworthy, assuring that she will receive the child's communications and reflect the child back to herself, establishing the self and the other in the interaction. Instead, in Vickie's mind her maternal object stands against her, obstructing her contact with the other and with herself. This dream proved to be a key to the map of her internal world, a selected fact (Bion, 1967) organising my understanding of her dilemma: contact with the other is fearfully resisted and desperately sought at the same time.

As Gregorio Kohon (1999) has written, these types of patients have turned away from the primary maternal object, both "prematurely and in hatred" (p. 80). This flight away spares the child from the pain of a mother who is physically present, but emotionally absent, in essence a "dead mother" (Green, 1986). The absence of the containing mother haunts the child, as an intrusive bad object, following Bion's (1962) idea that the absent good object is a present bad object. Distancing from an intrusive object is possible only through exile of the needy child-self, and an identification with an omnipotently ideal object.

Kohon continues (1999), saying:

> The *premature turning away* from the primary object was accompanied by the creation of a self that was idealised as all-loving and good, but which apparently did not need anybody or anything. Any dependency is later experienced as an act of humiliation perpetrated by the object; in the context of analysis,

any interpretation of the patient's needs represents an attack on the integrity of the self. (p. 80, original emphasis)

Like many patients with a similar history, Vickie felt threatened when I moved towards attending to the split-off parts of her experience by suggesting she needed her mother. Then, she collapsed into a sea of despair about never being good enough, and the impossibility of contacting and holding her shameful, needy, child self. Her reliance on an identification with an ideal self for salvation required her to cut off huge parts of her alive and vital self, essential for growth and engagement with others. Alienated from herself, and without positive links to coordinate her internal world, she operates without a compass or a map, and cannot help herself by moving and travelling within herself to access different parts of her experience.

Vickie's narcissistic retreat in her tree serves as a protective shield for her deficient self that is unformed and unrelated to (Symington, 2002). The phantasy of a robotic repair masks deficiencies and "psychical holes" (Green, 1986, p. 146) that remain beyond sight and out of reach. Seeing herself as the victim of her mother's callous indifference, her identification with an indifferent object erects a barricade of anger, warding off knowledge of the deficits she harbours inside, and the "needy" despicable parts of her she cannot get rid of. At the same time, her retreat into a narcissistic world of no-objects, where time stands still, leaves her unable to mourn and therefore to develop new links to herself and to her objects. The dream shows Vickie's valiant quest to protect her mother, keeping her below and away, while remaining invisible, preserving her hope that her mother is a good mother. Ascending towards the powerful ideal, she attempts to summon her mother, imploring her to change at the same time.

The destruction of meaningful communication of emotional pain in Vickie's family was vividly described by Vickie as a rule that nothing was to be said about her mother's cutting-out or disappearing. The family reinforced a private belief system, organised around idealised sacrificing. If everyone sacrificed, the mother could be saved, and all would be well. This sacrificing called for sustaining a high level of masochistic suffering, elevating the most vulnerable dependent person, her mother, above all others. Vickie took on this role believing that through her scapegoat identification she could swallow and absorb all suffering, relieving her parents, and over time, her suffering would gain her more. This is the idealised side of the scapegoat dynamic. Her sacrifice would in the end elevate her above the mother she saved. In her unconscious, the sacrifice she made would transfer into being loved in the way she desperately longed for and needed: more attention, more care, more love. The family ideal of masochistic suffering was meant to compensate for the paucity of maternal love.

Bion (1962) equates maternal love with reverie and he writes: "For example, when the mother loves the infant what does she do with it? Leaving aside the physical channels of communication my impression is that her love is expressed by reverie" (pp. 35–36). In the following description the mother is used to denote a primary maternal object which could be mother, father, or another caring adult in the child's world.

The mother's process of minding her infant, her attunement to her baby's non-verbal communications, the quality of her responses, her tone of voice, and timing, transmit to the baby her love for and delight in the baby's being. Bion (1962) describes maternal reverie as a form of emotional digestion, such as a bird masticating food for her chicks. Receiving her baby's distress, the mother "digests" her baby's discomfort, soothing the irritation or pain, returning a palatable emotional state for her child to take in and use. In this way, maternal functions activate links and the linking processes in the baby, links between the internal world of the baby and the object world, between bodily experiences, and a mind that understands and responds, between a need and an object capable of meeting that need (Bion, 1962).

Reverie requires the modifying object, the container, to tolerate the child's distress, to take it in and feel it, without judgement, or blame. A mother containing her child's pain feels this pain as if it were her own, connecting deeply with it, drawing on her own experiences (Grotstein, 2007) in thinking about, imagining, and feeling the painful state clearly enough to be able to name it. The maternal function, as the myth of Isis portrays, gathers the pieces, puts them together, to understand, to see, and to assemble the child's self. In my experience, reverie begins as a liminal process, at first barely perceptual, gradually moving from a feeling to a thought, weaving the threads towards an emotional awareness, an element of meaning linking to other meanings of the interactions in the session. Piece by piece, an understanding takes shape out of the formless, preverbal experience, now suffered and thought about by two minds and the unfolding process occurring between them. In this way an embryonic awareness evolves as the foundation for the conception of a subjective self.

Without enough maternal containment, to sooth and to affirm the child's self, a type of "chronic reverie-deprivation" (Ogden, 2005, p. 59) can set in, affecting the aliveness of the communication between the therapist and the patient. When in these moments, we, as therapists, feel the "zone of non-existence" (Davoine & Gaudillière, 2004, p. 12) in our patients, and in ourselves. The zone of non-existence stems from the child's experience of the maternal object's lack of reverie, felt by the child as a sadistic attack against the essential being of the self (Symington, 1983) resulting in a penetrating and torturing agony. While a tolerable dose of the lack of maternal containment is necessary for development, a sustained, chronic, and pervasive lack of maternal reverie becomes in the child's mind a hostile judgement against the existence and aliveness of the self. The mother's indifference, and absence of care, takes shape in the child's mind as proof that the self is worthless and unlovable, a parasitic link, cutting into the self, as Vickie described. In these cases, the mother's unconscious hate is not known or represented by the mother, and is transmitted nonverbally, through actions and projections. Reacting to these transmissions, and in the midst of an internal firestorm, the child incorporates a maternal object who, the child unconsciously believes, loves another child better. And in addition, the child feels as if she should not exist, exerting a strangle-hold on the self.

I suggest the killing of the alive self takes place through the scapegoat identification. The child fights against the haunting painfulness of the mother's hatred as perceived by the child. To bridge this gap, the child reactively banishes parts of the self that attest to the existence and separateness of the self. The scapegoat mechanism operates under a series of "rules" and prohibitions the child implements in an effort to match the imagined ideal of the mother. The mother, unaware of this state of affairs in her child's internal world, appears to the child as a functioning mother, capable of loving but remaining indifferent to the destruction taking place in the child's inner world.

Patients with this internal dynamic bring an identification with a deadness inside them into the therapy relationship. Vickie felt sure she could not trust me to receive, recognise, and understand her scapegoated and alive self. Subsumed in the negative L link of indifference and the negative H link of revenge and blame, Vickie wanted me to affirm her goodness rather than attend to the raging, alone, and frightened parts of her. Trapped in the net of a double bind, she desperately longed for recognition of herself, yet refused to accept the castigated scapegoat self, demanding, instead, acknowledgement of her pristine and perfect self. As a result, she felt unwanted and unloved and without access to her whole self—both loving and hating parts—and could not know herself without integrating these two drastically different emotional experiences. What does it take to stop the internal scapegoating of the self? How does a negative H link shift and transform towards a positive link, propelling further thinking, understanding, and development, activating realisations and integrations, giving birth to an authentic self?

Holding Vickie's dream image in mind, I kept the memory of her as a lonely, hating child, up her in tree, stuck and dependent, and thought of the cut rope as a rudimentary "proto-mental" (Bion, 1948, p. 101) seed that could potentially germinate into a positive link. Vickie's hatred, once noted, documented, and suffered, could become a positive link. As André Green (1986) posits, the technical demands of working with these types of patients goes beyond the challenge of interpreting the hatred. Of paramount importance is a requirement for the therapist to remain alive, in the domain of positive linking activities, through reverie, and alive within to the "central decathexis of the primary maternal object" (Green, 1986, p. 146), and the "blank" space at "the primary core of this constellation" (p. 146). At times, images came to my mind of a black hole, consuming matter into nothingness, or a faulty computer, unable to light up and activate the mind. In response, enlivening images came to mind, such as the Milky Way on a dark night, or a spring of water surging out of the ground near a tree, or an empty cupboard with many shelves, a rudimentary structure to hold things.

When Vickie turned away from her damaged, hungry self, just as she felt her mother sadistically turned away from her, I turned towards images of the furious infant-self, helpless and without words, starving and utterly dependent, refusing to climb down from her treetop. At times, my hatred of her wish to cut out, rather than to integrate, rose up inside me. Irritation with her relentless litany of self-castigation and resentment towards others, including me, threatened to catapult me out of my therapeutic frame of mind, destroying any empathy I might find for her. I fought to retain my capacity to think, refusing to scapegoat myself as the pitifully inadequate therapist, unable to sufficiently give her what she needed. Instead I reminded myself of her refusal to accept herself, and her resolution to fix her objects, rather than to find the fragmented and dispersed parts of her and use her innate capacities for synthesising to build meaning for herself.

I came to recognise the gaps, the stops, when Vickie would stutter or stop talking, as linked to herself stuck in the tree, trapped, feeling I did not care, and she did not matter. Only one person was in the room in these moments. I felt alone and realised there is no way I could know where she went. Sometimes the sound of my voice broke the silence, helping her to come back. She would start abruptly, break off again, nod her head without saying anything. I imagined she felt she did not matter to her mother and assumed I felt uninterested in her. This reflected her disinterest in herself, her indifference to the small experiences of everyday life she cut off that potentially held meaning for her. Perhaps she thought her mother was better off without her and, following this assumption, she imagined she protected me from her harm. I thought she must contend with killing off her identification with her mother in order to give birth to herself.

Case description

After several years of therapy, Vickie started the next session by saying she noticed she was leaving work on time, no longer staying late, so that she had time to go to an exercise class or buy groceries before going home. Still anxious about taking this time for herself, she felt some pleasure in knowing that she could leave, and even though her boss might not like it, he would not hold it against her. This marked an internal shift in her, having described many years of compulsively working 12-hour days and weekends. Recognising herself and her needs, rather than waiting up in her tree to be seen, I felt something had softened between us. Continuing, Vickie quickly said she feels tired and drained. Nothing she does is good enough.

Noting her despair immediately after she described her act of self-recognition, I thought she reverted to the scapegoat mechanism to recover her safe position up in the tree, looking down contemptuously on herself, in reaction to her internal shift giving her permission to take more for herself. This tactical retreat from herself appeared to protect her from the gains she took, and the potential for more contact with others, indicating her continued reliance on immobilising herself through an internal scapegoat ritual.

Saying more, Vickie started to cry, holding her face in her hands, despairing of ever being herself. She wants to be herself, to feel herself and know it is really her. She is constantly telling herself she is guilty, and she is to blame. Even though she is an adult, Vickie remembers always thinking that her mother must have been right not to love her, and that this fact had to do with there being something wrong inside her. Recognising the import of this statement, she suddenly stopped and looked at me, making eye contact. Repeating her statement, Vickie affirmed her belief in this reasoning, seeing at once that logically this did not make sense, yet feeling at some deeper level it must be true.

Vickie believes that the failure of maternal containment resides in her and this belief functions as a type of sacred belief, unquestionable and untouchable, and provides a stepping-stone to survival through engaging her inner resources to atone for her guilty failure. The meaning of her life then revolves around her belief that her sacrifice outwitted her mother's indifference, restoring health and loving impulses between them. The simplicity and power of her statement took my breath away, and I desperately wanted to convince her of the falseness of this belief. Her tears revealed a sadness and despair, indicating that she is beginning to see that her wish to fix her mother through sacrificing herself cannot provide her with the sustenance she needs.

I said: "You took a step forward for yourself and then drew back, yet you want to find a way to be yourself without feeling guilty."

She said: "I don't know how to stop that. I don't know what to do. I can't help that little girl up in the tree."

Having distanced herself from the frightened little girl I thought she feels the thrust of her sustained scapegoating. I say softly: "You want to feel yourself on solid ground, with room to move around. Climbing down seems terrifying."

She says: "Sometimes I am not sure she is still there. I am afraid to find out."

She is silent and turns away, seemingly ashamed. Devoid of any contact with others, she fears she is responsible for having killed the little girl part of herself through her prolonged and crippling isolation. She seems aware of her self-hatred, and of her shame for her needs and feelings of emptiness, and for having clearly cut off a dimension of herself.

Going on she says, quietly: "Nothing changes. After all I have done for my mother, I thought she would get better and give me what I needed. That never happened. If that little girl climbs down from the tree, I feel I will have nothing. All is lost." Here is a different kind of sadness, less an angry protest than a recognition of her losses. Once she saved her mother, she thought she could go back and pick up her life where she left off, and her sacrifice would stand as a debt to be repaid (Riviere, 1936). But that never happened. Now, in order to live, she must give herself the chance to be alive, but she feels this is wrong. If she takes life for herself, she unconsciously feels she will kill off her damaged internal mother. How can she possibly survive that?

Her face trembles and tears come to her eyes. She stops in a state of trepidation. Then she says angrily: "I don't know what to do with this. I don't want this on my shoulders." Sensing another cutting-off of herself, a minus link and signpost of her trauma, I say: "Perhaps you feel I am detached, not seeing you, up in the tree, blaming you rather than helping you climb down." She says: "It is not your job to help me climb down. I am to blame for not coming down. If I feel terrified it's my problem."

I say: "You feel you need my help, and this is terrifying in itself. You stay safe by staying away and going it alone."

She says angrily:

> I don't even consider blaming you. I am better off alone. I don't need anyone. That is safer. If I need something it is always on me. I get consumed with figuring out what I need and if I am right or wrong. If I take something, I feel I am taking it away from someone else.

Describing her internal scapegoat ritual based on assigning blame, she feels she has no other recourse. Who is to blame for her feelings? Is she at fault, or has someone she loves failed her? Must she absorb her painful feelings or is she justified in attributing them to the other?

She remains silent, suspending thought, and I think this is a sacrificial moment when a prenatal thought could be gestated, or, equally possible, could be sacrificed again. Stopping the scapegoat identification opens the question of the veracity of her belief system based on blame. Her aliveness could dissipate the shadow of her mother's absence and, thrown into this empty space, she might feel overwhelmed, unable to claim herself.

She wants me to help her get down into herself and seems to realise she must do this for herself. The moment of tension around her wish to feel alive collides with her wish to wait for the impossible while remaining safe. Suddenly she breaks the silence and says: "I feel you are listening to me. But I have nothing inside. There is nothing to say. I am afraid of coming down, and I think you will be angry with me, and disappointed."

Rather than cut out the pain or take it away, I think Vickie conceives of the possibility that she might be terrified and at the same time full of a painful desire to know and feel her aliveness. Sensing a pregnant moment and reaching for a new link that could perhaps be helpful to her, I say:

> Perhaps if you come down into yourself you will feel you angry with me, for standing separately from you. If you are in yourself with your feet on the ground you will be in yourself, feeling you are really you.

She looked at me with a shocked expression as if seeing something for the first time. She said: "I have always had to make sure others like me and want me. I have never thought of the possibility that maybe I did not want them."

Discussion

Distancing from herself and turning away from her subjective experience, and what she feels inside, relying instead on objective reasoning, she makes a case *for* or *against* herself. This judging, blaming activity discredits her internal experience, contrasting her experience within herself against the image of her ego-ideal-self: a pristine, all-good girl, without anger, hatred, or rage. Perceiving the discrepancy between what she should be, according to her ego-ideal, and what she feels she actually is, she remedies the gap through adopting the position of an "other" in herself and judging herself accordingly. Taking the position of objective judgement represents a form of negative linking, protecting her from the splintering pangs of shame and guilt for failing to measure up to her ideal. The ideal rises above her true self, abandoning the little girl cut off from others, in favour of a false identification, complete and untarnished by separateness. She hates herself for not being perfect, for her dependencies and deficiencies. But substituting an ideal image of herself does not deliver the necessary nutrients for building a genuine self, based on her own experiences and the truth of her point of view, distinctly hers.

Vickie feels she is chronically stopped in time, at a stand-still. Not able to use her linking capacities, she cannot move out of her fixation or free herself from blame. She feels at heart as if she has nothing. How can she stimulate the muscles and bones of herself into movement and action, purpose and resolve, moving her inside, along her highways and byways, mobilising autonomous linkages for herself? How does therapy enliven the organising capacities of her mind, linking the memories of her abandoned child-self, the child shut out, as well as linking to the capable professional woman, taking hold of her life and enjoying herself?

Positive H links unleash fears of destructive, murderous hate, as well as vulnerable feelings of separation, aloneness, and possible banishment. Accepting the reality of Osiris' death, Isis resolves to affect a proper mourning. She acts resolutely, affirming her loving feelings for him, and facing the destructive power of Set. Without denying his violent, unjust death, Isis determines to create, conceiving and giving birth to a son, a generative act, the outcome of her mourning. In comparison, negative H empowers an absolute, untouchable, and unassailable self, beyond contact, like the robot in the sci-fi story. But the robot, programmed to kill, can only repeat the same act over again, until dismantled by those who designed him. The movement from negative linking functions to positive ones requires a purposeful "internal act" (Symington, 2017), a resolve to shift the focus away from an ideal object, towards human frailties and the realities of being human.

Perhaps Vickie relies on my determination to find her, and gather her splintered pieces, in order to gain the courage to suffer the recognition of her spilled blood, and the consequences of her rage and hatred. Separation brings sorrow, for the loss of love and for the frightened angry child residing within her. Along with this realisation comes the recognition of her turning against herself, and the blame exercised against herself. These desperate measures add up over time and cannot be undone. She pays the price of having scapegoated herself, and thrown herself into fixing her mother, a delusional wish purchased at the expense of herself.

Stopping the scapegoat identification calls for Vickie to relinquish her control through blame and resentment, reversing the process of disowning herself, retrieving and accepting the banished parts of herself, engaging in creating herself from within (Symington, 2002). The recognition and acceptance of her destructive hatred contains the potential impetus for movement towards mourning, catalysing a positive H link. By positive H, I mean a link affirming and defining Vickie as a separate person, with her own point of view, thoughts, and experiences, distinct and specifically hers. Knowing positive H links provides a measure of cohesion for the self, and grasping, holding, and feelings of hatred connect to tender feelings of love and care, gone amiss. Hatred as a positive link can be used to push off identifications with an indifferent maternal object or a distant, ideal object, contacting instead a creative, life-giving source inside the self (Symington, 2002), knitting together emotions, experiences, and thinking in a stable narrative, locating herself within her experiences and solidifying a subjective self with a particular history and meaning.

The etymology of the word "hate" traces back to the Greek word "kedos", meaning "care, trouble, sorrow", and the Welsh word "cas", meaning "pain, anger" (Online Etymology Dictionary). The origins of the word shed light on the experience of hate linked with sorrow, care, and pain. Hate has to do with a lost loved object, with the L link. The reference to "care" seems to signify the "care" and attention that hate commands, and the care, or effort necessary to develop the capacity to tolerate hate interwoven with loving feelings. As Steiner (1993) writes, if the subject "can retain sufficient contact with his psychic reality to acknowledge both his hatred, which leads to the wish to destroy the object, and his love, which makes him feel remorse and regret, then development can procced" (p. 77).

Experiences of positive H heat up the numb, deadened self. Just as a mother dog will lick her pups immediately after birth to awaken their skin and nerve endings, the positive H link enlivens the connective tissue of the body–mind system, proving the existence and value of the genuine self. Potentially, my wanting to know Vickie, the K link, recognising and hearing from the little girl up in the tree, stimulated Vickie's wanting-to-know and wanting-to-feel her genuine self.

Positive H effects contact with a separate other, and the courage to survive confrontation and the communication of one's position in relation to the loved person. Positive linking activities promote the taking back of projections and split-off parts of the self, strengthening the core self. An indecisive, disgruntled despair, at first vague and unsettling, if accepted and allowed to permeate the body–mind, and attended to by the therapist—actively suffered and put into words—stimulates the integrative functions of the self. Once put in motion, positive links fuel the ego's engine, heating up integrity and curiosity in oneself, forming possibilities for growth and fulfillment. Positive H gives courage and authority to refuse the scapegoat identification, promoting a sturdy refusal to accept the other's image of oneself.

Progress was made in the moments when Vickie could feel and express her anger towards me. In these moments I held, as resolutely as she did, her hatred towards herself, and her mother, now expressed and felt towards me, attempting to give myself time to properly categorise the hate, to suffer it and understand it, and to reposition it within a positive linking matrix. Positive links arose out of the ashes of lost loved objects, and uncatalogued experiences, not suffered, registered, or documented within the self. Linking activities gradually coalesced Vickie's sense of self through reviving her experiences, giving them specific shape and meaning, attending to the painful gaps, deficiencies, and limitations within her, and between us.

I suggest that the scapegoating of the self is a form of negative H, and the task of therapy is to reach into this painful and violent attack against the self, motivating a movement towards positive H and positive links accepting the self, with all blemishes, limitations, and failures. This requires an inner act of acceptance of the self (Symington, 2002), without judgement, no matter how vile and destructive the self might seem to be. As Symington (2002) explains:

> The core difference between condemnation and acceptance is that in the former the negative qualities in the personality are hated and expelled from it with violence. ... Acceptance, on the other hand, receives the negative quality, and through that very act the quality becomes endowed with a positive valence and becomes a source of strength in the personality. It is a principle that anything that stays in relation to all others is good, whereas if it becomes separated or isolated, it has a corrupting effect upon the personality. ... What needs to be emphasised is that in the act of acceptance it is the act itself that structures both our system of perception and our beliefs. (p. 21)

Unconditional acceptance of the self opens the way to positive linking functions, if the challenge is taken to gather up the splintered and fragmented parts, hold them long enough to feel, shape, and describe the contours of each piece, and mourn the damage done to the child-self ruthlessly banished. Accepting that pain is part of being alive, and in being alive one feels pain, opens the way to find more contact with reality, relieving tormenting revenge, and the chronic suffering of self-blame. Vickie fought against accepting that life is the way it is, and she is in life, but she can't control it or the world she was born into. Receiving and holding the frightened and deficient parts of herself, as well as her destructive hate, Vickie began to realise that she would need to kiss the beast inside to take responsibility for her choices and to claim herself. Stopping the scapegoat identification, the hatred turned against the self in a negative H defensive activity, must be contained by the therapist and held, until such time as the patient can begin to see the damage perpetrated upon the self and take back the investments in the ideal object, reclaiming the hatred in its positive form. In this way the scapegoat identification also requires the therapist to kiss the beast inside herself, and to hold the truth of her hatred as part of the work of therapy.

A scapegoat identification creates a false hope based on the substitution of an identification with an ideal object in the place of the subjective self and under the guise of magically fixing the needed object. Functioning effectively as a safety net against the painful emptiness inside, the scapegoat identification, at the same time, prevents the self from proceeding towards accepting the realities of oneself as a whole person with both loving and hating emotions. Substituting an identification with the ideal is not the same as having an alive self in relation to an alive, limited, and perhaps damaged, other. Positive linking functions bring us into an alive, tumultuous, and sometimes frightening emotional world, always in flux, breathing, moving, dying, and being born.

CHAPTER THREE

Documenting parricide:
Abraham, Isaac, and Hans

Paul Koehler

> But Jesus said, 'Suffer the little children, and forbid them not, to
> come unto me: for such is the kingdom of heaven.'
> —Matthew 19:14

In his thoughtful and deeply disturbing book, *In the Shadow of Moloch: The Sacrifice of Children and Its Impact on Western Religion*, Martin Bergmann devotes a section of one of his chapters to Abraham's sacrifice of Isaac. There he cites, among others, a work by the American sculptor, George Segal:

> In our time the American artist George Segal has made a sculpture called Abraham and Isaac. The sculpture is pared down to the very essentials. There is no altar, no ram, no restraining angel. Only an older man with a knife and a younger man on his knees, with his hands tied, ready to receive the blow. Not even his legs are tied. There is nothing to keep him from getting up and running away. The sculpture was intended to commemorate the massacre at Kent State University. In the hands of a sensitive contemporary artist the Abraham myth has been transformed: all that is shown is the intergenerational hostility and the willingness of the child to be sacrificed. (1992, p. 114)

I was able to locate a picture of this sculpture on the internet. I had thought that it must have been included as a part of the memorial at Kent State itself, but I found that it is now on the campus of Princeton University. It is entitled simply: "Abraham and Isaac, In Memory of May 4, 1970".

Several things struck me about this sculpture, foremost of which was the position of the knife in Abraham's hand. It is held at exactly the genital level, as if to suggest almost a sense of an equation between the father's penis and the knife he is about to thrust into his son. I found another picture of the sculpture from a different angle in which there initially seems to be confusion—or, at least, ambiguity—as to whether or not the protruding, phallic shape is indeed the father's penis.

This brought to mind the drawing by Rembrandt on the cover of Bergmann's book. Rembrandt's Abraham seems to lack the steely resolve that is on the face of Segal's Abraham, but still, as Bergmann notes, Rembrandt's Abraham shows "no sign that this distasteful act is no longer required of him [but] on the contrary he looks bewildered, as if an act to which he was totally reconciled has now been countermanded" (1992, p. 114).

Here also, though, Rembrandt has Abraham holding the knife at the same latitude as the genitals, and in this drawing the knife is held at an angle suggesting an erection.

The other thing that struck me about Segal's sculpture was that, as Bergmann notes, Isaac has assumed a position of submission—and even complicity—in his own sacrifice. Although his hands are tied, they are not positioned as if he intended to protect himself. Rather, they are below his own waist as if to cover—one senses, not so much to protect as to hide—his own genitals. At the same time, his chest seems thrust forward and his head is tilted back, as if to offer his father a choice as to where to stab him. And, as Bergmann notes, although his legs are not tied and he would thus be free to run away, he is nonetheless on his knees.

The link between the knife and the penis suggests several things to me. Is there something in Abraham—in all of us—that feels somehow guilty that we are able to procreate—to create life—at all? In that act—in that capacity—are we somehow usurping God or the gods, stealing from them some of their power and, in so doing, opening the door to who-knows-what punishment? Do we then feel compelled still to give to them, in some fashion, our first fruits, just as in past epochs we offered up the first of our children or the first of our crops in order to preserve their continued good favour?

I also wonder if, in some part of our unconscious, we hate the link between sexuality and death, and therefore hate our children—who are, after all, both the fruits of our procreativity and the embodied reminders of our mortality, in a sense made urgently necessary by that very mortality.

It seems now relatively easy to consider the Abraham and Isaac story in terms of what Bergmann calls the Laius complex—that is, the hatred in the prevailing generation towards the generation that is or will be rising up to replace it. It is perhaps more difficult to recognise how the story, especially as depicted by Segal's sculpture, carries some suggestion, some representation, of the reluctance of the rising generation to claim and to engage the aggression—I would say even the violence—necessary to replace, to steal life from, the prevailing generation.

With that in mind I think we can then imagine Isaac's complicity as the result of the projective identification of just that aggression and violence into Abraham; which is to say that Isaac, having disowned the aggression and violence that stealing life *from* Abraham would require, can then only offer up the fire of his life *to* Abraham, and so submits willingly to *his* knife and *his* fire.

In his paper, "The waning of the Oedipus complex", Hans Loewald (1979) writes, rather uniquely I believe, of the violence, and the consequent guilt, that I am considering here. Loewald emphasises the intergenerational forces that press upon and affect the resolution—or the non-resolution—of the Oedipus complex. In Loewald's view, the Oedipus complex involves the child's confrontation and collision with the power and the authority that currently—for him—reside in his parents (and beyond them in the larger community and culture), but that will eventually fall to him as he is able to develop and claim that power and authority for himself.

Loewald goes on to suggest the price the child must pay for the stealing and the appropriating of parental authority: "In the Oedipal struggle between the generations, the descendants' assuming or asserting responsibility that belonged to the ascendants arouses guilt in the descendants (although not only guilt)" (1979, p. 389).

It is worth noting at this point the somewhat paradoxical or antithetical meanings of the words "ascendants" and descendants". "Ascend" means, literally, to climb up; "descend" means to climb down. We speak of our descendants as those who come after us. As a rule we don't usually say we hand life *over* to them; instead we most often say we hand life *down* to them. So, life *descends* from us to them. But in terms of the cycle of the generations, those descendants are actually *ascending* towards the power, the authority, and the responsibility of adulthood, while we, the so-called ascendants, are necessarily *descending*—waning as it were—well ahead of our descendants, towards death.

Loewald also notes the two meanings of the word "responsible"—that is, the sense of being responsible for the conduct of one's life and the sense of being responsible for—that is, guilty of—a crime. He writes:

> In considering this from the particular angle I wish to emphasise it is no exaggeration to say that the assumption of responsibility for one's own life and its conduct is in psychic reality tantamount to the murder of one's parents, to the crime of parricide, and involves dealing with the guilt incurred thereby. Not only is parental authority destroyed by wrestling authority from the parents, but the parents, if the process were thoroughly carried out, are being destroyed as libidinal objects as well. (1979, p. 389)

This murder starts out so minutely, so benignly, and so incidentally that it is hardly noticed as such: we learn to feed ourselves and to walk without assistance; we learn how to dress ourselves and to tie our own shoes; we learn how to read and to explore the world on our own; we learn how to compete in a sport or to play an instrument. With each of these little successes, these little victories, these little murders, we sever a part of our dependence on our real or symbolic parents and we claim an increasing responsibility and an increasing authority for ourselves. What goes mostly unnoticed—but which I expect is always registered unconsciously—is that with each of these accomplishments we are, in psychological fact, stealing life from our parents, and in that stealing seemingly moving them ever closer to decline and death.

It is useful here to consider the etymological connection between the word "success" and the word "ancestor". Both words come from the Latin "cedere", which means to go or to move. There is an implication in the word that in that going or that moving, something has to yield or give way. Our English word "cede" carries that part of its meaning. "Succeed" means, literally, to go or to move next or after. "Ancestor", then, means one who goes or moves—and then yields—before. These words seem to underscore Loewald's point: it is by way of these accomplishments, these little successes, that we become the successors of our ancestors.

How is it that we are able to manage the guilt inherent in "murdering" our parents—in *making* them ancestors—and ascending to become their true descendants, while at the same time positioning ourselves to become the ancestors of—which is to say, to yield and give way to—the coming generation?

Beautifully elaborating—and, we might say, also murdering and transforming—Freud's (1924d) notion that the superego is the heir of the Oedipus complex, Loewald writes:

> The organization of the superego, as internalization or narcissistic transformation of Oedipal object relations, documents parricide and at the same time is its atonement and metamorphosis: atonement insofar as the superego makes up for and is a restitution of Oedipal object relationships; metamorphosis insofar as in this restitution Oedipal object relations are transmuted into internal, intrapsychic object relations. (1979, p. 389)

As I understand it, Freud's idea was that as the oedipal child starts to imagine the consequences to himself of continuing to challenge and compete with the greater powers of the parents, he decides to yield to those greater powers and begins to identify with the rules and values of the parents, and in that way begins to establish that internal structure, the superego. Here I want to highlight that Freud seems to emphasise that it is the need to *submit* to parental authority—we might say, it is the need to *attenuate* aggression and violence towards parental authority—that drives and inspires the formation of the superego.

Loewald, if not completely standing Freud's idea on its head, at the least elaborates the other side of the coin: it is the psychic murder of the parents and the gradual appropriation of their authority—not simply the giving way to their greater power—that not only makes way for but in a certain way necessitates the formation of the superego. That is, in Loewald's view, the guilt we feel for stealing life from our parents and becoming "responsible" for ourselves is atoned for by the formation of the superego. That which our parents did for us—as well as the particular and distinctive ways they did those things—is replaced by an internal structure of our own making that limits, protects, guides, and inspires us. We take in their rules, their traditions, their values, and their ideals, and we at once transform them and make them our own. Our particular and deeply personal transformation of those rules, traditions, values, and ideals—that is, our particular metamorphosis of who they are and then of who they were—becomes the core of who we are and of who we strive to become.

Thomas Ogden, in his discussion of Loewald's paper, elaborates the importance—and the appropriateness—of Loewald's use of the word "metamorphosis". In a compelling analogy he likens the process of superego formation that Loewald is describing to the metamorphosis of a caterpillar into a butterfly. Ogden notes that while the DNA of the caterpillar and the butterfly is identical, the physical structures of the caterpillar are broken down and transformed into something new that is in fundamental ways quite different from what it had been:

> The parents (as experienced by the child) are not internalized, any more than a caterpillar sprouts wings. The child's "internalization" of oedipal object relations involves a profound transformation of his experience of his parents (analogous to the breakdown of the bodily structure of the caterpillar) before they are restituted in the form of the organization of the child's more mature psychic structure (superego formation). ... In other words, the child's "internalized" oedipal object relationships (constituting the superego) have their origins in the "DNA" of the parents—that is, the unconscious psychological make-up of the parents (which in turn "documents" their own oedipal object relations with their parents). At the same time, despite the powerful transgenerational continuity of oedipal experience, if the child (with the parents' help) is able to kill his oedipal parents, he creates a psychological clearance in which to enter into libidinal relationships with "novel" [Loewald's word] (non-incestuous) objects. (2009, pp. 127–128)

I like the conciseness and the economy of Ogden's phrase "psychological clearance": "if the child ... is able to kill his oedipal parents, he creates a psychological clearance in which to enter into libidinal relationships with 'novel' (non-incestuous) objects." Ogden goes on to elaborate that by this he means a freedom to pursue relationships with others in ways which, while partially coloured by oedipal transferences, are not dominated by them. I would extend this notion of psychological clearance to include also an authorisation and a freedom to inhabit and to pursue one's own life in one's own way.

In Loewald's view, then, the superego, this internal structure, is the result and the representation—the document—of both a parricide and a metamorphosis. At the same time, this internal structure, carrying as it does the particular and unchanging "DNA" of our oedipal object relations, also documents atonement and reconciliation, in that it is by means of the DNA that makes up that structure that we remain "at one" with our parents and most deeply remember them. It is our passport for leaving them behind and for carrying life forward beyond them; and it is the way we carry them with us.

And, as Loewald suggests, when we freely offer ourselves—that is, when we freely offer our values, our ideals, our limits and prohibitions, our guidance, our traditions, our particular wisdom, our deeply felt ways of doing things— when we offer ourselves in those ways to our actual or symbolic children, both to steal from us and to transform us, we grant to our parents, indeed to all of our ancestors, a kind of immortality.

Loewald goes on to describe how the superego might develop when the crime of parricide is not fully accomplished and one feels unable to tolerate, to atone for, and to transform the guilt of that felt crime. He writes:

> Need for punishment tends to become inexhaustible if atonement or reconciliation is not eventually brought about by mourning (the word "atone", literally and in many contexts, means to become or cause to become *at one*, to reconcile, to bring concord or harmony). (1979, pp. 389–390)

Here we can make a useful distinction between suffering and sacrifice. Although the inexhaustible need for punishment that Loewald is noting clearly entails a kind of continuous suffering, I would suggest that that suffering might be better understood as a repetitive sacrifice rather than as a proper suffering of the psychic pain of guilt and mourning which might lead to atonement and reconciliation and then to increased autonomy and further growth.

We can imagine, then, that in those cases, the superego has not developed as a consequence of atonement for a true parricide but rather that its structure carries and reflects a failure or at least a side-stepping of that psychic act. Here we can imagine George Segal's Isaac as representing that part of the self that retreats from parricide, that recoils from engaging the violence necessary to steal life from Abraham and chooses instead to incorporate, rather than to transform, a vengeful, God-like Abraham who demands, inexhaustibly, a repetitive sacrifice.

Guilt and mourning then go unsuffered and so do not gain sufficient strength, do not gain sufficient momentum, do not gain sufficient urgency— we might say that guilt and mourning do not gain sufficient *life*—to promote metamorphosis, growth, and generativity. Instead, that psychic pain is short-circuited by way of a sacrificial propitiation, often of the very parts of the self that might seek to grow and to prosper, a propitiation whose purpose seems instead to be the sustaining of an omnipotent, a timeless, and in many ways a lifeless, status quo.

As a way to provide a framework for thinking about the ways in which this psychic pain may be either suffered or propitiated, I would like to refer to Roger Money-Kyrle's paper, "The aim of psycho-analysis", in which he suggests that a primary goal of psychoanalysis—and, we might add, of an intensive psychoanalytic psychotherapy—"is to help the patient understand, and so to overcome, emotional impediments to discovering what he already knows" (1971, p. 442).

Money-Kyrle follows Bion (1962) in the presumption that we carry certain preconceptions, preconceptions which, if met with appropriate and tolerable realisations in the course of development, can then be recognised, understood, yielded to, and, finally, internalised as abiding truths of our existence. These pre-conceptions, these truths, then become, in Bion's terms, conceptions, or, we might say, guiding principles that constitute both the container and the contained of our life-long journey of emotional growth. That is, they help to form and to structure—in a sense to define and refine—our understanding of the parameters, the limits, and the boundaries of our lives, and also to inform and to elaborate our understanding of what might be imagined, conceived, nourished, and sustained—brought to life— within those boundaries.

In his paper Money-Kyrle cites three preconceptions as having primary and particular significance and which, as well, are often met with emotional impediments to their discovery: "the recognition of the breast as a supremely good object, the recognition of the parents' intercourse as a supremely creative act, and the recognition of time and ultimately death" (1971, p. 443). Loewald's understanding of the act of parricide can be fleshed out to include overcoming the emotional impediments to the discovery, the suffering, and the acceptance and internalisation of those preconceptions.

We can imagine that, in certain respects, the human infant begins to suffer the recognition of the breast as a supremely good object from the very moment he leaves the needlessness and the timelessness of the womb. As we know, the extent of the disruption and even the trauma of that transition will be softened and ameliorated by the kind of welcome he receives. As Joyce McDougall (1980), among others, has observed, it is the task of the mother to "seduce" her infant into life, such that the infant can tolerably accomplish that transition—that crossing of the boundary—from prenatal to postnatal life. This seduction will include the mother continuing to provide something akin to the "heaven" that the infant experienced while still in the womb. This provision serves not only to ease the transition into postnatal life, but it also provides a storehouse of narcissistic capital for the infant to rely upon as he gradually achieves a transition from the pleasure principle to the reality principle.

The mother's seduction then initially entails helping the infant to continue to experience his illusion of omnipotence while also gradually to suffer the disillusionment of that omnipotence and in so doing to cross the boundary of that omnipotence and to begin to apprehend the world around him and his place in, and his relation to, that world.

Winnicott (1945) describes the first experience of the infant—the first apprehension of the breast—as being characterised by omnipotence, hallucination, and illusion. Blissfully unaware of his smallness, his vulnerability, and his frailty, the infant's initial experience of himself, if all is going well, is as if he himself were what he would later understand to be God. Although he does not yet have the words for it, his experience must be something like: In the beginning *I* created the heavens and the earth and *I* separated the seas from the dry land, and *I* saw that it was good.

This illusory experience of omnipotence is made possible by his mother's ordinary devotion, what Winnicott calls her "primary maternal preoccupation" (1956). In his paper, "Primitive emotional development", Winnicott describes what he calls the moment of illusion thus:

> the infant comes to the breast when excited and ready to hallucinate something fit to be attacked. At that moment the actual nipple appears and he is able to feel it was that nipple that he hallucinated. So his ideas are enriched by actual details of sight, feel, smell, and next time this material is used in the hallucination. In this way he starts to build up a capacity *to conjure up what is actually available*. ... it is a mother's job to protect her infant from complications that cannot be understood by her infant, and to go on providing the simplified part of the world which the infant, through her, comes to know. Only on such a foundation can objectivity or a scientific attitude be built. ... Only on a basis of monotony can a mother profitably add richness. (1945, pp. 152–153, my emphasis)

"Monotony" here suggests some sense of slow rhythm, of needs being experienced and then quickly satisfied, but as yet no real sense of passing, measurable time.

In describing the ending—really the gradual evaporation—of the period of illusionary omnipotence, Winnicott is in a sense describing the first loss the infant suffers, a loss foreshadowing the eventual weaning and indeed each subsequent loss that is yet to come. He famously describes the mother's necessary state of mind as being almost an illness, and he adds, "I bring in the word 'illness' because a woman must be healthy in order to recover from it as her infant releases her" (1956, p. 302).

I want to note especially the words "recover" and "releases". What is it that permits and compels the infant to release—to liberate—the mother and himself from their symbiotic union? Here it is useful to remember Melanie Klein's assertion that for the infant "the breast is instinctively felt to be the source of nourishment and, in a deeper sense, of life itself" and, as she goes on to say, "the good breast is taken in and becomes a part of the ego, and the infant who was first inside the mother now has the mother inside of himself" (1957, p. 178–179).

What Winnicott is suggesting is that if the breast is initially present enough, satisfying enough, and apparently omnipotently controlled enough, and then gradually and tolerably ceases to immediately appear when summoned, then that gap, that absence, that disillusionment of omnipotence can be registered, recognised, and suffered. Ownership of the breast can be remembered and mourned, mourned and remembered, allowing the infant to establish that external breast as an internal object. The infant begins to feel: I am *not* the breast, but now I do have some of its goodness inside me. Perhaps we could say that the mother recovers her "health" and her prior sense of consciousness—which is to say, her prior sense of herself as a separate object—as her infant begins to destroy and mourn his prior sense of omnipotent control and ownership of her.

I link the words "remember", "destroy", and "mourn" deliberately here. Roger Money-Kyrle describes it this way:

> To what extent the internalization of the first good object is the same as establishing a concept, it may be hard to say, but at any rate the capacity to mourn or pine for a loss and the capacity to remember the lost object are inseparably linked. Without the memory there can be no mourning and without the mourning there can be no memory. (1971, p. 444)

I would add to this that without the giving up—which is to say the *destroying*—of omnipotence there can be no lasting internalisation of the breast and without sufficient internalisation of the breast there can be no lasting destruction of that omnipotence. It is important to emphasise that the remembering, the destroying, and the mourning that we are considering here are parallel, synergistic internal processes, which is to say they are deliberate, if largely unconscious, psychic actions.

Using Bion's (1962) terms we could say that the infant comes into the world with a preconception of the breast as a good and nourishing and vital object. When the infant in fact encounters a realisation of that preconception, when he encounters a breast of sufficient and even ample availability and abundance, this realisation then becomes a preconception of what else might be further realised in his life. This preconception would manifest itself in a sense of vitality, and also in a growing sense of confidence and resilience, and a beginning sense of faith that the world—and his life—can potentially be abundantly satisfying, that one can indeed conjure up what is actually available and can find the psychological clearance to exercise what Christopher Bollas has called a "pleasure in being" and to cultivate a genuine and enriching sense "of gratitude toward life—for what it offers and how it can be *taken*" (Bollas 1995, p. 92, original emphasis).

The infant's release of the mother will also signal—as well as permit and encourage—his continuing to turn away from omnipotence and starting to turn towards reality. That is, it will signal the first stirrings of his desire to recognise and to respond to the dangerous snake of otherness, and to begin to desire to explore, to take in, and so begin to *know*—as opposed simply omnipotently to have and to own—that otherness, first in the person of his mother and then in the world around him. The infant's release of the mother then will begin provisionally to document the first stirrings of parricide, if at this point only in his simply taking in, which also is to say, *taking*, life from his mother.

And as the breast becomes less immediately—which is to say, less omnipotently—available, the infant begins to learn to wait and also to realise he is *able* to wait, and with that to enter and to begin to inhabit what Thomas Ogden (2005) has called "the externality of time" (p. 97). As omnipotence recedes and is destroyed, a nascent sense of competence and, especially, an anticipation of competence, will begin to emerge and to seek realisation.

In her paper, "Acting on phantasy and acting on desire", Hanna Segal suggests that even though initially the infant is necessarily under the sway of the omnipotence associated with the pleasure principle, the reality principle, in terms of a nascent capacity to turn away from omnipotent phantasy and towards objective reality—to recognise what is actually available—is present if only in a rudimentary way, from the very beginning of life:

> an infant that obeyed only the pleasure principle could not survive, whatever the care of the mother. Were he satisfied with the hallucination, he would refuse the food and care of the mother, since the latter never comes up to the ideal expectation. The infant has to tolerate such discrepancies, and his capacity to recognise an object that is not identical to his phantasy and to relate to it, is the basis of his maturation. From the beginning of life the infant is faced with the choice of testing his phantasy against reality—letting reality modulate his phantasy or attacking reality—that is, primarily attacking and destroying his capacity for perception. The extent to which the infant can tolerate reality depends both on his inner capacities to tolerate frustration and on the degree of frustration or satisfaction provided by the environment. (1992, p. 106)

In their book *Fearful Symmetry: The Development and Treatment of Sadomasochism*, Novick and Novick elaborate the importance of the mother, especially her alive and responsive presence, in facilitating the infant's turning away from the omnipotence of the pleasure principle and turning towards the actually available pleasures and competencies promised by the reality principle. The mother's almost absolute responsiveness to her infant, as well as her vitality and the palpable delight she takes in that infant, serve both to gratify and to confirm his omnipotence while at the same time provide the seeds for what will later become his experience of competence and mastery.

> Ordinarily, the child's real capacity to elicit the appropriate response from the care-giver is the root of feelings of competence, effectance, and reality-based self-esteem. The capacity of the mother–infant couple to repair inevitable breaches in the empathic tie is an equally important source of feelings of competence and positive regard. A range of positive feelings from contentment to joy becomes associated with those competent interactions and comes to instigate, reinforce and signify empathic interaction. Thus pleasure is dependent upon and regulated by the capacity

of each partner for realistic perception and interaction with the other, which leads in turn to the experience of having an actual effect on the other. (1996, p. 53)

We can imagine then how those beginning pleasures in competence—those first pleasures in "the experience of having an actual effect on the other"—go hand in hand with a beginning experience of "pleasure in being", and how the initial accumulation of those pleasures could contribute to the infant's willingness to release his mother from their symbiotic bond.

Novick and Novick are suggesting, then, that the experience of that pleasure begins—and in a certain way is made possible—at the point at which, paraphrasing Segal, the infant can begin to suffer the discrepancy between his hallucinatory phantasy of an ideal mother and his growing recognition of his real mother, whom he can competently interact with but cannot quite omnipotently control. The experience of magically conjuring up what is actually available slowly modulates and transforms into the capacity to achieve—that is, to bring about through his own efforts—what *might* be possible. That pleasure in competence, then, will serve also as a buffer and a comfort against the disillusionments that are yet to be suffered: at rapprochement, during toilet training, during latency and adolescence, and beyond.

It becomes necessary then for the mother, as Janine Chasseguet-Smirgel has observed, to balance gratifications with tolerable frustrations:

> Carefully dosed frustrations and gratification serve to encourage the child to give up certain satisfactions, linked to the acquisition of certain functions and to a certain 'way of being', in order to acquire new ones. Each stage of development must afford him sufficient gratification for him not to be tempted remain at that stage (to be fixated), in short for the *hope* that will allow the child to continue to climb the steps of his development to be sustained. (1985b, p. 30)

Chasseguet-Smirgel is suggesting that when the mother's dosage of frustration is within sufficient and tolerable limits for the infant—when there is, initially, abundant gratification and then, gradually, both sufficient gratification and yet also enough frustration to engage a process of disillusionment—this will encourage in the infant a gradual turning away from his feeling of and reliance upon omnipotence and a gradual turning towards reality as well as a nascent feeling of confidence about moving on with his development. Reality then begins to beckon towards further growth rather than simply to threaten his omnipotence. The capacity comfortably to wait for the reappearance of the breast begins to modulate into the capacity comfortably to anticipate, and even to desire, the next stages of development. And, as Chasseguet-Smirgel suggests, the infant begins then to cathect the process of development itself.

Novick and Novick go on to describe what can happen when, in the development of the masochistic patients they treated and studied, frustration overshadowed satisfaction and that initial sense of pleasure, competence, and hopefulness did not sufficiently take root and grow:

> When our patients were infants, their inborn capacities to elicit needed responses were often ineffectual. All the masochistic cases were intermittently loved and cared for, but in a way that undermined confidence in their ability to evoke a response. Their wide-eyed gaze was not met by a mother's adoring, joyful look, but by a blank, depressed deadness. Their mothers smiled when they emerged from their depressed or anxious state and felt like smiling, not in response to the child's smile. The only constant in their unpredictable lives was the experience of the range of dysphoric feelings so, as Glenn (1984) and Valenstein (1973) have noted, these patients came to associate their mothers with pain. As one patient said, 'Unhappiness is the smell of home.'
>
> Under the impact of such extreme and frequent disappointment, these patients turned away from their inborn capacities to interact effectively with the real world and instead began to use the experience of helpless rage and pain magically to predict and control their chaotic experiences. The failure of reality-oriented competence to effect empathic attunement forced the child into an imaginary world where safety, attachment, and omnipotent control were magically associated with pain. (1996, p. 53)

Novick and Novick are suggesting that these patients, at the very beginnings of their lives, did not properly experience themselves as God. That is, they did not sufficiently experience the illusion in which the gap—the discrepancy—between the suffering of need and the satisfaction of that need was narrow enough to be almost unrecognised. Instead they experienced—abruptly, prematurely, and overwhelmingly—their vulner-ability and helplessness vis-à-vis the "otherness" of life. At best, then, there was only a reluctant and begrudging turning away from the mother and towards reality. For these patients, the larger world did not beckon so much as threaten to intervene still further between themselves and the unrealised mother of their omnipotence, for whom they still seem to be searching. Development and maturation, and in a certain way time itself—that which would take them still further away from the mother and towards a greater engagement with reality—then would, understandably, be something to be resisted, denied, refused, or undone.

Novick and Novick's observations confirm Fairbairn's (1943) premise that the infant will need to preserve a sense of a good object—and a sense of a benign, benevolent, gratifying, and secure world—at virtually any cost. And so, when he encounters frustration in his interactions with the mother, when he experiences her lack of responsiveness, her indifference, or the absence of her delight in his being and his capacities, he will not be able objectively to suffer the recognition of those failures and shortcomings. Unable to bear what he might otherwise be able to see, he will instead sacrifice a part of his capacity to see. In lieu of perceiving and registering his mother's "badness", he will instead take that badness into himself, enlisting his unrequited omnipotence into the attempt to magically detoxify that badness in the endopsychic theatre of his internal world.

As Fairbairn (1943) noted so cogently: "It is better to be a sinner in a world ruled by God than to live in a world ruled by the devil". In many ways these patients do seem, overtly, to consent to being sinners in a world ruled by God. At the same time, embedded in their self-sacrificing sinfulness, their unrequited omnipotence persists, functioning as a hidden, rageful, and envious god, too hungry and furious to accept the discrepancy between their phantasies and desires and the actual world they find themselves in.

This infant god who was first inside the mother suffers from not yet having a sufficiently life-giving and nurturing mother inside of himself, and, as Fairbairn suggests, this becomes an absence that cannot be mourned. Instead there will be a melancholic identification with the indifferent, the antagonistic, or even the hostile mother that he is not able to recognise. Not having been sufficiently seduced into life, not having sufficiently experienced the pleasure of competently gaining the mother's attention, affection, and delight, this infant god will not find the psychological clearance to cultivate the gratitude for life that would both allow and enable him to recognise what might actually be there for him to conjure, to take, and to make use of. In other words, in the absence of an initial experience of competence there will be little willingness to cathect the process of development, and instead the pursuit of immediate, magical, and self-sacrificing solutions will tend to prevail.

Money-Kyrle makes the point in his paper that

> [w]here there has been a favourable development, and the concept of the first good object is well established, together with the capacity to remember it with love, there is far less difficulty in being able to recognize the parental relation as an example of the innate preconception of coitus as a supremely creative act—especially as this is reinforced by a memory of a good relation between the nipple and the mouth. (1971, p. 446)

With this in mind we can better appreciate why Klein (1928, 1945) believed that the Oedipus complex has its beginnings in and is set in motion by—in a sense is "released" by—the frustrations of weaning at around six months. Whether or not actual weaning occurs at that time, certainly *by* that time, if development has gone well, the infant has begun to experience and hopefully to tolerate a gap between his need and wish for the breast and its actual reappearance, and in that gap—in that waiting—has begun to have, and to mourn, some sense of is otherness. As Hartocollis (1983) has noted, it is the infant's capacity to remember the breast in its absence that provides his capacity to expect its reappearance and so to develop a provisional sense of the future, a provisional sense of Father Time: the breast is not here now; it will be here soon.

Initially, as Klein sees it, the absent breast is experienced as a present, persecuting breast, which then becomes associated with a rudimentary phantasy of the mother and the father together, enjoying all the pleasures and satisfactions which at those moments are being denied to him. The bad breast and the bad, depriving couple are envied, hated, and attacked. As Mrs Klein elaborates in her 1945 paper, "The Oedipus complex in light of early anxieties", as the depressive position is worked through, the child mobilises phantasies of repairing and restoring the damaged breast and the hated parental couple. Both the breast and the parental couple are recognised as life-giving and necessary for survival. The child, out of love for both the mother and the father, yields to the father's prerogative, and to his greater capacity, to repair, to satisfy, and to sustain the mother. This helps the child to further relinquish—to further release, to further destroy—his omnipotent, dyadic union with the mother.

This dawning recognition of the mother's "other" life will gradually yield to the recognition of generational differences and generational boundaries. The young child will soon see and grow to understand, if not immediately accept, that his parents have a relationship with each other that is different from that which he has with each of them. He will see that he is separate from and excluded from—that is, "other" from—that relationship. As his omnipotence further recedes and is further destroyed, he can bear to rewrite Genesis: *I* did not create *them, they* created *me*!

While the loss of the breast initially "releases" oedipal frustrations and conflicts, it is, as Money-Kyrle (1971) suggests, the preceding internalisation of the breast that allows the child to bear "the recognition of the parents' intercourse as a supremely creative act". If that recognition can indeed be properly suffered, it will open the door for the child to begin to identify with that creativity, the very creativity that brought him into being. That initial sense of competence in being able to prompt and secure the mother's responses and delight—in having "the experience of having an actual effect on [that] other"—will grow into the confident capacity to desire, to compose, and to create and sustain a life for himself within the boundaries of the world in which he finds himself.

The parricidal destruction of the child's omnipotence will be transformed and sublimated into the active pursuit of—and, more importantly, the willingness to suffer—his own development. The aggression and rage that are evoked by the disillusioning of his omnipotence may then be mobilised in the service of that very parricidal intention. It is as if the child says, both to himself and to his parents: I see—and I hate—that you are older and bigger and wiser than I am; I now will put my efforts to the task of becoming an adult myself. The earlier capacity to suffer the absence of the breast, with a growing confidence that it will soon return, may then yield to the growing capacity to suffer time, practice, and growth in the service of achieving, of attaining—of *stealing*—the capacities and prerogatives of the parents.

As I noted, Loewald suggests that it is by way of mourning that the guilt of parricide is worked through and atoned for. However, he does not elaborate what that work of mourning entails. If we hold in mind what psychoanalysis has taught us about the process of mourning, it should help us to imagine and to think about how one mourns—or fails to mourn—the many losses, both for oneself and for one's parents—that are inherent in the stealing and the appropriating of life that Loewald describes.

In "Mourning and melancholia", Freud describes how in normal mourning the process of encountering and recognising the absence of the object is repeated again and again. He writes:

> Each single one of the memories and situations of expectancy which demonstrate the libido's attachment to the lost object is met by the verdict of reality that the object no longer exists; and the ego, confronted as it were with the question whether it shall share this fate, is persuaded by the sum of the narcissistic satisfaction it derives from being alive to sever its attachment to the object that has been abolished. (1917e, p. 255)

I understand Freud to be saying that it is by way of this *descent* into the psychic pain associated with the repetitive confrontation with the absence of the lost object and, subsequently, the gradual withdrawal of libido from that object, that the mourner then "allows" the object to die. If mourning is to be completed and resolved, this allowing will need to be a deliberate internal action—a "severing"—which suggests a consenting to the fact of the loss of the object, rather than a passively experienced recognition. Then, and only then, is the mourner able to return—we might say, to *ascend*—to the reality that includes the absence of the object and to being fully alive once again. This return—this ascent—then may be accompanied by some sense of enrichment and gratitude, for having had and known the now lost object and, I think, also for the now deeper understanding of the parameters, the limitations, and the sufferings that are inherent in life, which is to say the life that the mourner himself still has. In those instances, it has always seemed to me, it is finally the *light* of the object—and not just its shadow—that falls upon the ego.

Conversely, Freud tells us, in melancholia the lost object is not allowed to die, but by means of an incorporative identification remains as a part of the self. The melancholic mourner remains burdened by—and in a certain way deadened by rather than enriched by—the lost object. Rather than suffering a return to the world of the living, he seems more to desire to follow the lost object into the ground, or into the sea, or on to the funeral pyre, as if those realms were preferable to—and more alive than—the human realm of the living.

In those instances, then, *only* the shadow of the object falls upon the ego. In one part of the melancholic mourner's mind, of course, the loss is indeed recognised and a terrible sorrow is felt. But at the same time, the pain evoked by the fact of separation from the object and the guilt over still being alive seem to preclude a full return to the ordinary satisfactions of living. The melancholic, then, seems to have made an internal decision to continuously sacrifice the part himself that wishes to and might still strive to return to the world of the living in order to deny the painful separation from the lost object and to propitiate what is felt to be an unbearable guilt over still being alive.

The guilt over still being alive has its antecedents in the oedipal situation, as the young child begins to confront and recognise generational boundaries and generational differences. The otherness of objective time that began to emerge in the oral period will now yield to the beginning recognition of the otherness of generational time—that is, that the parents' and the child's lives exist in separate if overlapping segments of time.

Even as the oedipal child suffers and mourns the loss of the omnipotence he experienced and enjoyed in his dyadic union with the mother, a loss that is confirmed and made evident by his awareness of his parents' separate and exclusive relationship, and even as he then strives eventually to achieve their capacities and prerogatives for himself, he will also begin to realise that they are "ahead" of him in time. As he mourns for what he himself has lost, he will also begin to mourn for the lives his parents eventually will lose as he himself ascends to replace them.

We could say that, if the oedipal child has had an insufficient, frustrating, or traumatic relationship with the mother, "the sum of the narcissistic satisfaction [he] derives from being alive" will not be sufficient for him "to sever [his] attachment to [her]" (Freud, 1917e, p. 255). He then will be unable to suffer and mourn for the dual realities of his separation from her and of the disillusion of his omnipotence. Similarly, he will be unwilling to mourn for the foreshortening—from his point of view—of his parents' lives. On the contrary, he will seem to want to deny or to try to stop time itself.

Freud suggests that the guilt over still being alive is intensified and complicated by any hatred or grievance that had been harboured towards the lost object. In a similar way, hatred and grievance towards the parental objects tend to intensify the guilt that would accompany the psychic act of parricide and complicate the mourning that would facilitate the resolution of that guilt.

In a series of chapters in his book *Seeing and Being Seen: Emerging from a Psychic Retreat*, John Steiner (2011) vividly describes the dilemma for the oedipal child—and for the adult who still carries that oedipal child—when there is an overabundance of hatred and grievance towards the parental objects. Steiner describes how, paradoxically, that hatred and grievance—of, course, often inspired by very real traumas, injustices, and injuries—can make it feel impossible to psychically kill those objects. In a certain way, they are hated far too much ever to be "allowed" to die.

On the one hand this hatred becomes so saturated with resentment and the desire for revenge that simply killing them—and getting on with one's life—is felt never to be enough. Where is the justice for all that was done to me, for all that I suffered? Rather than a completed parricide, there seems instead to be a perpetual torture of the parental objects while at the same time a perpetual sacrifice of the vital parts of the self.

On the other hand, the hatred of the parental objects, and the consequent desire for revenge, evoke the potential for such a degree of guilt that a sense of grievance must be sustained indefinitely as a defence against that guilt, a guilt that makes the prospect of actually completing a proper parricide feel impossible to bear.

It is as if that hatred and that grievance and that guilt have irradiated the oedipal DNA and created some inflated, malignant mutation. Now a different kind of document emerges: instead of a butterfly, the superego becomes something more like a fire-breathing dragon. This superego does not document a grateful atonement for stealing and carrying life on beyond the parental objects but rather institutes and sustains a perpetually punishing and hateful fusion with those objects.

Steiner makes the point—and I think it is an important if somewhat neglected point—that the discovery of the primal scene, of the parents' separate and exclusive relationship, is *always* experienced as an injury, shattering as it does the prior sense of an omnipotent, exclusive possession of the mother and leaving in its wake, always, some sense of resentment and grievance:

> Knowledge of the psychic reality of the relationship between the parents is felt as a blow to omnipotence that is tantamount to a castration threat from a malignant powerful father motivated by hatred and envy. Such castration threats may lead to the dissolution of the Oedipus complex, as Freud (1924) described, but they leave behind a deep sense of injustice and violation that fuels the wish for revenge. The child feels that he is forced to give up his incestuous wishes toward the mother because of his father's cruel authority, but he does not recognize the justice of this demand. Although he may redirect his sexual desires and inhibit his hatred and vengeance, he is left with feelings of grievance which make

> him look forward to a time when he can enact revenge and achieve
> the Oedipal gratification he has been denied. (2011, p. 134)

Some of our most troubled and difficult patients, as we know, have still not recognised the justice of the father's demand. Instead they seem to have constructed—and to have become trapped in—a dark "family romance" (Freud, 1909c) organised around grievance. As Steiner notes, in their grievances they have remained preoccupied with a sense of injustice for what they feel has been denied to them, done to them, or taken from them, a preoccupation often taking the form of an endless chronology of events of their lives in terms of what should have been and what should not have been. In a certain way they never quite face "the verdict of reality" as to the actualities of their own histories, and the particular consequences of what did and did not happen for and to them. That is, as Steiner describes, a superego judgement concerned with morality overshadows, and defends against, an ego judgement concerned with reality.

This is another way of saying that one cannot psychically kill, and then mourn for, one's parental objects until one has fully recognised that one has had the parents, and the life, that one actually has had. Implicit in that recognition is the deflation of oedipal omnipotence as the oedipal child yields to, as he *concedes* to, both the actuality and the justness of the parental relationship—I would emphasise here, of that *particular* relationship— that excludes him, that preceded him and, impossible as it may seem, that created him.

Implicit also in that deflation and concession is a beginning recognition and acceptance of what the Greeks call one's "moira" (Greene, 1944)—the "portion" of life that one is fated to carry—which, as their ancient and ever-timely literature demonstrates again and again, not even the gods can change. The recognition of the primal scene, then, and the recognition of the unalterable facts about one's life and by extension about reality itself, go hand in hand.

Steiner makes the useful distinction between what he calls the paranoid outcome and the depressive outcome of the Oedipus complex. In the paranoid outcome the oedipal child does not fully "allow" his omnipotence to die, and therefore he does not fully recognise the need to psychically kill his parents by the gradual appropriation of their power and authority. He never quite yields to the sense of smallness and helplessness and relative limitation that he is starting to experience and to discover about himself and his relation to the larger world. He, of course, does submit to the parental objects, but *only,* in his mind, because he was forced to and with an accompanying sense of a burning and humiliating victimisation. The differences between the generations—represented by the presence of the father and embodied in the exclusivity of the parental relationship—are disavowed.

When the oedipal child is able to relinquish his omnipotence and to yield to and to tolerate the experience and the discovery of his smallness, and then to begin to suffer the long journey of appropriation, the outcome will have a more depressive quality. He will not only recognise and accept his primary objects in their particularity, but also—especially when there have been injustices and traumas—he can begin to recognise, with some sense of proportion, the "verdict of reality" as to just how limited was his capacity to influence, to control, to change, or to heal those objects. When those limitations, that relative helplessness, can be realised and acknowledged, he then can begin to mourn not only for the stealing of life from his parents but also for his suffering of the particular injuries that were contingent upon his fate: for what did and did not happen, for what was present and what was absent. Now a superego judgement about morality can yield to an ego judgement concerning his actual reality.

Implicit in the depressive outcome of the Oedipus situation is the respectful—we might even say the reverent—recognition of the parents' intercourse as a supremely creative act. As Money-Kyrle (1971) suggests, if the breast, as the representative of life, has been satisfying enough for the child to be able to suffer the recognition that the breast is separate from himself, beyond his omnipotent control, and necessary for his survival—that is, if it has been sufficiently satisfying for it to be mourned and remembered, destroyed and internalised—the child will then be better able to suffer the recognition of both the exclusivity of the parental relationship and the supreme creativity of that relationship.

When love and gratitude hold sway over hatred and the wish for revenge and triumph, the child will wish to reverse and repair his attacks on the parents and especially on their creative link to one another. That reparation will then allow him to restore and establish a similar link in his internal world, making that creative link available now for realisation and further elaboration in his own particular ways. That is, by way of suffering that parricide, by way of making the parents' creative link into something of his own, he will establish the psychological clearance to establish a beginning authorisation for his own creativity to grow and to flourish, including but not limited to the freedom to seek and to find a novel object—a creative partner—for himself.

That psychological clearance becomes more difficult to achieve in cases where there was felt to be little in the parents that was worthy of identification or where their link to one another was otherwise not strong, and in cases where the actual biological parents were not known. Here the complicated psychological task is to differentiate the antipathy that is felt towards those objects from the recognition of the sacredness of their creative link—the link that gave one life.

If that differentiation cannot be made, and when hatred and the wish for revenge preclude a recognition of the sacredness of the parents' creative link, the oedipal child will feel dissuaded from the task of appropriating, trans-forming, and claiming such a link for himself. The shadow of his hatred will fall upon his own capacity to be fully creative, curtailing his freedom to engage in a mature sexual relationship with a novel object and truncating the aggression and the gumption necessary to sustain and succeed in creative pursuits in all areas of his life. This would manifest itself in a quality or a state, more or less, of non-consummation and non-fulfilment. Ordinary creativity in almost any form would tend to remain—or to deteriorate into—a sterile potentiality, never to be fully conceived, nurtured, and brought to life as *something*: projects are started but not completed; new skills go unlearned; degrees are not completed; dissertations are never written; relationships begun in great passion wither in the absence of devotion.

The shadow of that hatred will also fall upon the capacity to form a potentiating alliance with one's therapist or analyst. Janine Chasseguet Smirgel describes that hatred succinctly:

> it is the hatred of life, the non-acceptance of the primal scene as liable to give birth to a child, and, consequently, the impossibility of forming a couple with the analyst so as to give birth to a child that would be themselves, re-created. I would like to add that, in such cases, suicide is always lurking in the background. (1985a, p. 116)

The lurking possibility of suicide in these cases could be understood both as the expression of, and the defence against, the recognition of not having satisfactorily consummated the available possibilities of a particular life.

Our English word "consummate" comes from the Latin "consummare", which is formed from "con", meaning "with or together" and "sumare", "to add or combine", from "summus", meaning "highest". Our closely related word "consume" is also closely related in Latin: "comsumere" comes from "con" plus "sumere", which means "to take, use up or waste". "Sumere" is derived from "sub", meaning "under" and "emere", which means "to buy or take". In both English and Latin the two words suggest the link between the consummating of one's life—that is, the taking, generating, and carrying forward of life—and the consuming of one's life in that very process.

It is useful to note here the antithetical meanings (Freud, 1910e) of the closely related prefixes "sum" ("highest") and "sub" ("under " or "below"), which parallel the similarly antithetical meanings of "ascendants" and "descendants". With these meanings and connotations in mind, we can perhaps better appreciate how parricidal aggression, in the sense that we have been considering it, must always be inherent in generative creativity of any kind.

In his book, *Love Relations: Normality and Pathology*, Otto Kernberg carefully describes how the aggression and antipathy towards the parental objects, born originally in whatever frustrations were encountered in the relation to the breast and then extended and elaborated in the encounter with the parents' exclusive relationship, become available to be enlisted in the later achieving of oedipal success—that is, in the establishing of a mature sexual relation with a novel object. Among other things, that aggression is necessary in order to overcome the prohibition against, and to enjoy the sense of transgression that is inherent in, that success:

> Basically, transgression includes violating oedipal prohibitions, thus constituting a defiance of and triumph over the oedipal rival. But transgression also includes transgression against the sexual object itself, experienced as seductive teasing and withholding. Erotic desire includes a sense that the object is both offering and withholding itself, and sexual penetration or engulfing of the object is a violation of the other boundaries. In this sense, trans-gression involves aggression against the object as well, aggression that is exciting in its pleasurable gratification, reverberating with the capacity to experience pleasure in pain, and projecting that capacity onto the object. The aggression is also pleasurable because it is being contained by a loving relationship. And so we have the incorporation of aggression into love and the assurance of safety in the face of unavoidable ambivalence. (1995, p. 24)

Kernberg's observations confirm Freud's (1905d) assertion that the finding of a love object is always a re-finding—that is, a re-finding of the primary object. To the degree that that finding is a re-finding, to the degree that one experiences the aftertaste of the original relation to the primary object, the prohibition against transgressing upon that object and its rival will be activated. If one has sufficiently destroyed, remembered, mourned, and internalised the original objects, then one will be better able to safely re-experience something of the original bliss that was present in the dyadic relation with the mother and to safely participate in a novel primal scene that is not too much in the shadow of the original primal scene from which one was excluded and forbidden.

To the degree that one becomes able to make and sustain a mature relation with a novel object, that re-finding will also be experienced as a re-losing of the original object. One understands that one is only re-finding the shadow of the original object and not that object itself, that that object and that stage of life are indeed gone forever. In that realisation the aftertaste of blissful omnipotence at the breast will give way to the foretaste of mortality as one inhabits the position of carrying forward life oneself. This simultaneous experiencing of the re-finding and the re-losing of the primary object may account for the sometimes confusing feelings of pain and sadness that often accompany the experience of falling in love and committing to a partner.

Here we come back to the link between sexuality and mortality and to the interlocking nature of Money-Kyrle's (1971) three facts of life. Just as "the recognition of the breast as a supremely good object" carries the seeds of "the recognition of the parents' intercourse as a supremely creative act", so that second recognition carries the seeds of "the recognition of time and ultimately death". The parents' intercourse is driven by the imperative to spawn a new generation and, in that very spawning, the parents now position themselves eventually to be eclipsed and overtaken by the very parricide by which they themselves were able to assume their position as progenitors.

The link between the working through of the Oedipus situation and recognition of time and ultimately death is embedded in the original Oedipus story, particularly in the riddle that the Sphinx poses to Oedipus as he makes his way to Thebes: "What being, with only one voice, has sometimes two feet, sometimes three, sometimes four, and is weakest when it has the most?" (Graves, 1955).

As Leonard Shengold (1989) has noted, the Sphinx has been thought to represent any number of things, especially the young child's primitive ideas both of the powerful primitive mother and of the parents in intercourse. In that way, the Sphinx can be thought to represent some sense of the first two of Money-Kyrle's primary truths. And of course, Oedipus does triumphantly solve the riddle: "Man … because he crawls on all fours as an infant, stands firmly on his feet in his youth, and leans upon a staff in his old age" (Graves, 1955 p. 344).

We could think of the riddle itself as carrying some notion of the third truth. The reference to feet in the riddle, of course, provides a link to Oedipus and his traumatic history, as his own feet were bound when his parents cast him out to die and whose very name means "swollen foot" and thus carries the reminder of that history. At the same time, the association of feet to locomotion suggests the task of actively walking away—we could say from both the primal mother and the parents in intercourse—and into one's life, to pursue one's own development and growth, through time, from the omnipotence of the infant, who has the greatest feeling of power when he is in fact the weakest, all the way to the elderly person who needs a staff to continue walking.

Symbolically, Oedipus' capacity to recognise and accept the linked realities of development and time and therefore to solve the riddle enables him to achieve a parricide of sorts: "The mortified Sphinx leaped from Mount Phicium and dashed herself to pieces in the valley below. At this the grateful Thebans acclaimed Oedipus King, and he married Jocasta, unaware that she was his mother" (Graves, 1955 p. 344).

In his paper Money-Kyrle (1971) wonders if that third truth—"the recognition of time and ultimately death"—is a preconception of the same magnitude as the first two. I believe that it is and that in certain ways it is foreshadowed by them. Just as the breast is first partially and then permanently lost, so also is life. And just as, during the working through of the Oedipus complex, we are faced with the gap separating our desires from our capacities, so as we get older we must face the gap between the boundlessness of what we had hoped to achieve in our lives and our sober awareness of what we actually have achieved and might still hope to achieve.

Probably most if not all of us have had the experience of time seeming to pass more quickly as we get older. I think that can be accounted for in part—but only in part—by our increasing capacity, as we age, to imagine and to take the full measure of even a long life.

But I also think that as we get older our deepening understanding of the finiteness of each thing that we do create and accomplish also drives home a deepening sense of the finiteness of our lives, of the numberedness of our days. With everything that we do, everything that we choose, everything that we create and accomplish, we realise that we are only achieving a something—an actual, a particular, a definite and finite *this*—which in some sense will highlight and proclaim the still potential, the indefinite and unrealised, the formless and infinite *that*, that otherness which will remain forever beyond us. This may account for the sometimes confusing feelings of pain and sadness that also often accompany significant achievements in any areas of our lives. Even at our most creative—in some sense especially then—we must yet again suffer our lost omnipotence.

It is useful here to consider the etymology of our word "suffer". It comes from the Latin word "suffere", which means "to bear, to carry or put under". "Suffere" also comes from the prefix "sub", plus "ferre", which means "to carry" (from the Greek, "pheren", "to carry"). The prefix "sub" has a variety of meanings and connotations, including: under, beneath, from under, almost, close to, up to, towards, subject to, in the power of, a little, somewhat.

The history of the word suggests the particular pain associated with the continuous deflation of our omnipotence as we strive to receive, to embrace, and to carry forward life: in certain respects we are always, at virtually all points in the life cycle, suffering from being under, being behind, and being subject to the otherness of generational time. This suffering becomes—at least potentially—even more palpable as we age and come more deeply to understand that life itself was here before we arrived, that it exists inside of us for a while but never allots to us everything we would have wished for, and then, like the withdrawn and unperturbed breast and like the parental couple that closes the bedroom door on us, it will eventually leave and exclude us and will continue on, indifferently, without us.

In her paper, "On the sense of loneliness", written at the very end of her life, Melanie Klein (1963a) poignantly describes how the quality of one's experience as an infant and then as an oedipal child will influence and shape one's capacity to tolerate the realities of time, ageing, and ultimately death. She notes the important links between experiencing and receiving pleasure from the primary objects early in life and the capacity to give back to loved objects—and to life itself—as one goes through the life cycle and, inevitably and increasingly, experiences life to be receding. Mrs Klein implies that gratitude, when it holds sway over envy, is a necessary condition for accomplishing and tolerating a successful parricide—that is, for the gradual stealing and internalising of life from the primary objects—and that generosity, the desire and the capacity to give back, is a consequence of that parricide.

She writes:

> A happy relation to the first object and a successful internalization of it means that love can be given and received. ... Enjoyment is always bound up with gratitude: if this gratitude is deeply felt it includes the wish to return goodness received and is thus the basis of generosity. (p. 310)

In words strikingly similar to Winnicott's, she describes how the early internalisation of the breast and the concomitant establishment of a capacity for enjoyment can serve as a buffer against the decline and loss that are inevitably experienced later in life:

> The capacity for enjoyment is also the precondition for a measure of resignation which allows for pleasure *in what is available* without too much greed for inaccessible gratifications and without excessive resentment about frustration. (Klein, 1963a, p. 310, my emphasis)

Mrs Klein goes on to describe how a successful working through of the oedipal situation—that is, an acceptance that the parents have an intimate and generative relationship with one another that the child does not share in or have with either of them—will prepare and enable that child, when he becomes an older adult, to cede those adult prerogatives to the ascending generation as he himself moves towards old age and death:

> A child who, in spite of some envy and jealousy, can identify himself with the pleasures and gratifications of members of his family circle, will be able to do so in relation to other people in later life. In old age he will then be able to reverse the early situation and identify himself with the satisfactions of youth. This is only possible if there is gratitude for past pleasures without too much resentment because they are no longer available. (Klein, 1963a, p. 310)

The capacity of the child to suffer and to overcome his envy for what he himself did not yet have and to find a grateful and a generous attitude towards his parents in the first years of his life then will inform his capacity and, in the later years of his life provide the psychological clearance, to cede what he no longer has to the next generation. This generous ceding of life will both document and serve as a final atonement for the many acts of parricide that contributed to the making and the enriching of his own life.

CHAPTER FOUR

Into the arms of the god-object: The seductive allure of timelessness

James Poulton

Introduction

Time is a great teacher, but unfortunately it kills all its pupils.
—Berlioz, 1856

Franz Kafka, in his last published story, "A hunger artist" (1922), describes an unnamed "artist" who devotes his life to giving exhibitions in which he starves himself before the public. The artist's performances are managed by an impresario, who limits them to forty days because, he says, audiences lose interest after too long of a performance. The narrator describes the artist's objections: "Why should he [the artist] be cheated of the fame he would get for fasting longer … since he felt there were no limits to his capacity for fasting?" (p. 247). The story follows the artist as he falls from fame and accepts a humiliating position in a circus menagerie, where he is placed in a cage, with other animals, with a fading placard announcing his art. As time passes, he draws less and less attention. Finally, when everyone has forgotten him and even he has lost track of the length of his fast, he is discovered, near death, hidden by straw on the floor of the cage. The circus overseer approaches him with unexpected compassion: "Are you still fasting?" he asks. "When on earth do you mean to stop?" "Forgive me, everybody," whispers the hunger artist, "I always wanted you to admire my fasting," but he then adds that his fasting shouldn't be admired. "Why shouldn't we admire it?" asks the kindly overseer. The hunger artist replies: "Because I have to fast, I can't help it." "What a fellow you are," says the overseer, "and why can't you help it?" And here Kafka delivers a most chilling rejoinder: "'Because,' said the hunger artist, lifting his head a little and speaking, with his lips pursed, as if for a kiss, right into the overseer's ear, so that no syllable might be lost, 'because I couldn't find the food I liked. If I had found it, believe me, I should have made no fuss and stuffed myself like you or anyone else'" (pp. 254–255).

In a recent article, Thomas Ogden (2016) offers a penetrating analysis of this last scene, describing the hunger artist as having been "reduced to omnipotence" (Ogden attributes this phrase to Bion) and having devoted his life, not to find opportunities to love and be loved, but to demonstrate his superiority over others, to retreat to an interior cocoon in which he remains safely self-aggrandised, all the while depriving himself of the food he would have "liked" had he allowed himself to overcome his repulsion. Ogden points out that the hunger artist, in response to "momentary, unbearable self-recognition, denies his membership in the human race—a species that requires food to live—and instead claims a place in a nonhuman world", in which he floats in "timelessness and meaninglessness". The tragedy of his life, Ogden concludes, wasn't that he couldn't find food to his liking. Rather, it lay in the fact that "having found it (and found himself), he rejected it and himself (as well as the awareness of both)" (2016, 129–134).

The experience the reader has when reading "A hunger artist" is paralleled by the therapist's experience of patients whose primary defence is to retreat (Steiner, 1993) to an internal, near-autistic state that collapses any liveliness—whether originating in themselves or their therapists—that might be marshalled to help them. This kind of patient, sometimes referred to as exhibiting a "negative therapeutic reaction", teases the therapist with the possibility of engagement in treatment, but soon disappears into omnipotent retreat, looking on the therapy with amusement, superiority, or disdain. Just as Ogden asks why the hunger artist had to "savagely assault that state of mind in which he was aware of having found the food he liked" (p. 134), and finds no answer from Kafka, therapists often wonder what motivates such patients to reduce themselves to omnipotence if the price they pay is a forfeiture of passion and meaning.

[Note: Although the term "negative therapeutic reaction" is commonly used in describing these patients, it is the consensus of the authors of this book that the term is, on the whole, misleading. The word "negative" implies that the patient is performing an act that undermines the goals and conditions of treatment. If, however, as we argue, patients perform these acts as repetitive attempts to protect from unbearable realities, then "negations" can actually be seen as communications of the unthinkable or unspeakable aspects of their experience. From this perspective, "negations" are actually "affirmations" of the purpose and aim of therapy: to make the unconscious conscious. Accordingly, we suggest that what has been described as a negative therapeutic reaction should be conceptualised as neither a reaction nor as anti-therapeutic. Rather, it should be seen as akin to other transferences, which are largely viewed as actions (not reactions) brought into treatment, if only unconsciously, to move the treatment forward. If we don't see ordinary transferences as reactive and anti-therapeutic, then the patient in retreat towards a god-object should be spared such denigrations as well, no matter how much the patient's stance *appears* to undermine the treatment.]

In this chapter, I will discuss three of the most notable characteristics of these kinds of patients: (1) their retreat to a "*god-object*"—an idealised internal object in relation to which these patients establish a stable and almost impenetrable internal sphere which protects them from pain, hate, shame, frustration, and loss, and from which they view the events of their lives with implacable remove and serenity, and with a self-righteous sense of their own goodness; (2) the *timelessness* accompanying this retreat, which is evident in their absence of concern or even awareness that they are living as though in a capsule, numbly, without vitality, emotion, or movement, and without a clear awareness of time whether in the form of planning for the future or remembrance of the past; and (3) the seductive and erotic countertransference temptation therapists feel, in the presence of these patients, to become the sole possessor of *desire*—chiefly for the patient to improve, but for other goals or objects as well—as though by doing so the therapist can magically penetrate the patients' inner sanctum and rescue them from the dispassionate and antiseptic way they are living their lives.

Because a particular configuration of family dynamics is central to the development of each of these three characteristics, I will, as I describe them, make some observations about these patients' familial histories. Most, if not all, of these patients emerge from families in which splitting and projective identification (in one or both parents) predominate, leading to restricted capacities for thinking and symbolisation, shared fantasies of danger, shared harshly judgemental superego functions, unmetabolised aggression, oedipal conflicts, suppression of individuation, and envy (or "mimetic desire"—Girard, 1977). These patterns typically predominate because of a history of emotional or psychological trauma in the parents, which in turn traumatises the children, leading them to develop an internal world full of absolute negatives—unforgiveable offences, monstrous emotions, condemnable parts of the spontaneous, independent self—against which their only defence is to withdraw (or surrender) to the idealised inner sanctum of the god-object, from which they deceive themselves into believing they have escaped the wrongs of the world and of the badness in themselves.

The retreat to the god-object

In our first session, Doug said he realised that his fear of being shamed and ridiculed had effectively paralysed him. The son of a wealthy father who died when he was three, Doug had not had to work throughout his adult life. "I've spent," he said, "almost thirty years doing nothing." He attended school but didn't graduate; he dated but hadn't "even thought of marriage"; and he'd never considered committing to a career. His descriptions of his daily activities—shooting pool, watching movies, playing video games, working out—were lifeless, and they reminded me of a series of grey shadows, with little differentiation or sense of movement. "I want to get my life kick-started," Doug said, "so I can accomplish something before I die."

He described a childhood filled with traumatic experiences. He remembered being terrified of his mother, a proper, distant woman whose regular explosions of rage and ridicule Doug tried to prevent by stifling the desires or opinions his mother wouldn't endorse, becoming almost ghostlike in his refusals to show his real self. Additionally, Doug was sexually abused by a neighbour between ages eight and thirteen, and though the neighbour used threats to silence him, he was already silenced by his shame over the erotic pleasure he felt during the abuse. Finally, Doug was bullied by classmates, beginning at age twelve, and he became "a pariah" in school. By fourteen, his performance faltered and he thereafter couldn't live up to the potential his high IQ seemed to promise.

The internal world of a patient in a traumatic retreat, such as Doug, is split in two. On the one hand is an ego-destructive "super-ego" (Bion, 1962), a demonic object that is the legacy of cumulative shaming experiences in childhood—the "envious stripping or denudation of all good" (Bion, 1962, p. 97)—and is linked to and productive of the bad, shamed, and inadequate self. To defend against his superego's attacks and the re-experience of the bad self, Doug had invested in being "good", which in his case required that he eject those aspects of self that would seek interaction with others and thereby subject him to danger by triggering their condemnations. Thus, Doug dispossessed himself of love, hate, aggression, desire, longing, fantasy, and even certain forms of language (which could function as rehearsals of interactions), in order to both create and find comfort in an unobjectionable good self—the other side of his internal split.

Two aspects of Doug's "good" self should be noted. One was that, for all of his efforts to rid himself of hate and aggression, his retreat to the passive, interior position from which he could feel he was good was nonetheless the result of hateful and aggressive acts. He himself was the most visible target of his aggression, since his elimination of emotion, initiative, and so on, constituted a sacrifice of himself, or at least of the agentic parts of self that would have sought to engage with others, find gratification, make meaning via intentional action, and organise the external world to conform to *his* desires and ideas. It is a striking aspect of patients in traumatic retreat that their goodness is achieved only through extreme acts of self-directed negation and aggression, and that their fantasied attainment of that goodness severs them from awareness of the internal torment that motivated the defence in the first place. The other targets of Doug's hate and aggression were even less visible to him, but evident nonetheless. By refusing agency, goal-directedness, or creativity, and instead insisting on compliant invis-ibility (which, as Winnicott observed, induces "a sense of futility ... and is associated with the idea that nothing matters and that life is not worth living"—1971, p. 65), Doug deprived others of himself and thereby exacted his revenge on them. This hateful withholding was originally aimed at his tormenters—his mother, neighbour, and schoolmates—in order to indict them for having forced him into retreat, but through projective identifi-cation it generalised to others, including his therapist.

A second, pivotal aspect of Doug's retreat to his good self is best illustrated by two sessions in our second year. Doug had been dating a woman, Laura, with whom he "thought" he could fall in love, but she precipitously ended the relationship, calling him a "loser". In the session after he received this news, Doug was filled with shame and hidden hatred, and paralysed by depression. He entered the next session, though, in an unexpectedly self-assured mood, with an air of calmness and self-satisfaction. He said he realised the shame he felt the week before really didn't "serve" him and he had "decided" to eject it. "I don't need it," he said, "so I just got rid of it. And I'm *just fine*." When I pointed out he had solved the paralysis of shame by retreating from it altogether, he answered, prickly and condescending, "No, no. You don't understand. I haven't *retreated* from shame. I've *ejected* it. I don't own it anymore. And I don't need anybody, especially Laura, who stupidly tries to make me feel it." He then sat back, self-assured, and repeated, "And I feel just fine."

An enlivened, embodied self is an appropriating self, fully engaged in a dialectical interplay with the external world, and fully participating— not simply in assimilating the world, but also transforming it, moulding it to confirm and conform to its own desires. It is not intimidated by such engagement, nor by the conflicts that may arise from its "object-instinctual strivings" (Kohut, 1972, p. 365; see also Jaffe, 1988). In contrast, the self in retreat, as was Doug once he felt the shame and injury of Laura's rejection, not only abandons all striving, convincing itself it needs nothing and no one, but it also accesses the "omnipotent narcissistic and often megalomanic part" (Rosenfeld, 1975, p. 223) of the self in order to attain an unbridgeable distance from the demonic superego, and thereby evade the torment caused by others and the monstrous and unbearable emotions it engenders (i.e. "the truth of internal and external experience"—Ogden, 2016, p. 20; see also Riviere, 1936). That Doug's narcissistic defence in this instance is similar to Green's (2002) descriptions of "moral narcissism" should not be overlooked. (According to Green, moral narcissism is based on "asceticism and the negativation of gratification", "the decathexis of drives", and leads to "states of futility, void, emptiness, anorexia, and extreme ideali- sation"—2002, p. 637.) But the aspect of this defence I'd like to highlight is not just Doug's ascetic omnipotence, but also his sense of triumph and his mood of self-assurance and serenity. It is here, I believe, that the particular psychic configuration of the god-object becomes most visible.

As mentioned earlier, by the god-object I mean an ideal or idealised internal object that offers protection, safety, and a righteous sense of goodness to the self. Additionally, the god-object provides a secure internal space from which the patient can express hatred of himself and others, as well as of the world itself, without having to acknowledge or bear respon- sibility for it. The god-object is similar, to a degree, to Melanie Klein's idea of a "good" object (1952), or the "good" part of the superego (1948; 1963b) that offers "internal riches and stability" (1952, p. 58), and that is created by internalising the loving, admiring aspects of the parent. But the god-object is more than just an approving superego, because it also bestows upon the individual the magic of religious omnipotence that is most apparent in the patient's self-righteousness, serenity, and sense of triumph. Likewise, the god-object shares characteristics with the concept of the numinous (Otto, 1923), which is associated with "mystical and meditative contact with the ineffable", and with the "belief that there is a God within us—as a component of our very subjectivity" (Grotstein, 1997, p. 318).

But while the numinous represents the means by which the individual gains access to growth-enhancing transcendence, the retreat to the god-object represents a pathological attempt to solve the problems presented by the realities of the world by bringing them to a halt in a cloud of remove, implacability, and denial. Patients who embrace the god-object seek only a simulacrum of numinousness—a "grayscale" version of "O" (Bion) or of the divine (Jung)—that, far from expanding their sense of themselves or the world, collapses their experience to a vanishing point, illuminated only by a false and near-psychotic assumption of the sacred righteousness of their retreat. Far from establishing mystical contact with the ineffable, these patients are all too similar to Steiner's description of Oedipus as portrayed by Sophocles in *Oedipus at Colonus*. Whereas in Sophocles' earlier play (*Oedipus the King*) Oedipus had merely turned a blind eye to the truth, in the later play he "turns to *authority, in fact divine authority*, and in this way gains the persuasive power and moral conviction which enable him to show a contempt for the truth" (Steiner, 1993, p. 129, my emphasis).

As Steiner's observation implies, it is important to remember that, in those patients who embrace the god-object, the radical nature of their retreat cannot be reduced simply to an investment in omnipotence (cf. Riviere, 1936; Rosenfeld, 1975). Narcissistic defences that chiefly rely on omnipotence are not always accompanied by self-righteousness and serenity. A practising clinician will regularly encounter patients who use such defences out of desperation or urgency, or out of a need to be admired for their unparalleled abilities, and the anxious and manic quality of their assumed omnipotence is palpable. In contrast, the patient who retreats to the god-object has found a realm of detachment from which they do not care about, and aren't disturbed by, their failure to garner admiration from others. These patients have found communion with something far greater than mere human objects, which, because of the patients' traumatic history, can never be the source of lasting satisfaction or contentment. The god-object, for them, is not an object suitable for an object relationship. Rather, it is akin to a soothing and all-encompassing ray of light that bathes the patient with self-satisfaction unmediated by the external world—all while the patient remains unperturbed by the desires and instinctual drives that so beset others.

The serenity-inducing and quasi-religious characteristics of the god-object have led some authors (though they do not use the term "god-object") to recognise that its origin lies beyond the internalisation of just the good or the good-enough parent. Grunberger (1989), for example, says that in the womb the fetus experiences prenatal cœnaesthesis— a state of near-perfection marred neither by conflict, desire, nor need, because the womb takes care of all metabolic, regulatory, and protective needs before they arise. After birth this cœnaesthesis experience "leaves sufficient traces for it to be fantasised as a state of *perfect bliss, absolute sovereignty* or *omnipotence*" (1989, p. 16, original emphasis). When the child then has to face conflicts of growth and development, all of which mobilise drive-related object relating, it may utilise these traces to create a fantasised "monad"—a "nonmaterial womb which functions as though it were material" (p. 3)—in which the illusion that the child can function apart from object relationships predominates. The chief characteristic of this "nonmaterial womb" is that the child feels safe within it precisely because drive, need, and emotion have been eliminated—just as in prenatal experience—and consequently no longer have to be negotiated or even thought about (see also Poulton, 2013).

Chasseguet-Smirgel (1986) elaborated on Grunberger's views by suggesting that the fantasied retreat to a nonmaterial womb represents a "primary desire to discover a universe without obstacles, without roughness or differences, entirely smooth, identified with a mother's belly stripped of its contents, an interior to which one has free access" (p. 77). The fantasy of the smooth mother's belly is motivated, according to Chasseguet-Smirgel, by an equally primal oedipal fantasy of destroying the father's penis and eliminating rival siblings, in order to negate disturbing reality:

> It is a question of rediscovering, on the level of thought, a mental functioning without hindrances, with psychic energy flowing freely. The father, his penis, the children represent reality. They have to be

destroyed so that the mode of mental functioning proper to the pleasure principle may be recovered. The fantasy of destroying reality confers on the fantasy of emptying the mother's belly its primordial role. It is the contents of the belly which are equivalent to reality, and not the container itself. The empty container represents the unfettered pleasure. (p. 77)

The fantasy of the empty container of the mother's belly—that is, the nonmaterial womb—comes the closest, in existing psychoanalytic literature, to what we mean by the god-object. As Chasseguet-Smirgel makes clear, this kind of "object" is only tenuously connected to a specific object, particularly since identifiable objects, such as mother, father, or siblings, are part of the problem the retreat attempts to solve. Instead, the god-object is an empty container, which nonetheless provides basic, primordial resources to its seeker. It is: the lap of the perfect mother who asks nothing of the child and simply wants him to rest in her embrace (cf. Winnicott's view that a mother's preoccupation (1956) with her infant in his earliest months leaves a lasting trace in his mind of the time when the world was under "magical control" (1951, p. 238) and his desires didn't need to be expressed, or even felt, before they were satisfied); the space in which the seeker floats freely, relieved of the necessity of interactions and the frustration and pain they entail; the solution to the harsh and demonic superego, because in its presence all precipitants of badness and shame (desire, emotion, aggression, individuality, and separation) are eliminated; the source of a perverted form of transcendence and universality, because to enter one must shed those aspects of the self that make one a concrete and particular individual; and the bestower of serenity, since a full communion with the god-object means that all care has been evacuated, and all sense of threat or need has been erased.

In a personality like Doug's the god-object functioned both to counterbalance his harsh superego and to provide protection for hidden expressions of hatred. To merge with the god-object meant he had vanquished, if only momentarily, the superego, along with past and present objects whose shaming helped create it. This process opened the door for Doug's rediscovery of the seemingly infinite and eternal state of serenity that he could only feel once he traded in his human objects— who, in their human-ness, injured, traumatised, and enraged him—for the embrace of the god-object and the freedom from want, desire, and obligation it provided.

The allure of timelessness

A patient's retreat to the god-object provides multiple benefits, from omnipotence, superiority, and serenity to cover for aggression and freedom from obligation. But the embrace provides something else as well, something that can be seen both in individual moments and in large swaths of the patient's life. This is the retreat into timelessness, which is linked to the god-object in the same way the timelessness of eternity is linked to our ideas of God and heaven. For centuries, philosophers of religion have claimed that an essential aspect of God, and of being near God, is that He or She exists *outside* of time, in an eternity without past, present, or future that is impossible for mere humans to imagine. It is not impossible, however, to imagine that humans might want to mimic such timelessness, and find heaven within themselves, and thereby escape the "time-bound created" world (Ganssle, 2017), which, with its "apportioned life-spans" (Plato, from *Timaeus*, quoted in Von Leyden, 1964, p. 40) and a "Being-towards-death" (Heidegger, 1927/1962) that continuously aims towards the demise both of the present moment and of life itself, seems to many patients to contain far more pain than pleasure.

In a 1972 paper, Hans Loewald described the *experience* of time in terms of "reciprocal relations between past, present, and future as active modes of psychic life" (p. 140): "We encounter time in psychic life," Loewald said, "primarily as a linking activity in which what we call past, present, and future are woven into a nexus. The terms themselves, past, present, and future, gain meaning only within the context of such a nexus" (p. 143). There are, of course, many advantages to be gained from linking past to present and future: such linking gives us memories of things like first loves, or anticipations of events like the birth of a child—all things that make life uniquely human. But there are also many reasons to attempt to *unlink* these temporal modes of psychic life. When our past contains unmetabolised and therefore unbearable traumas, we are motivated to disconnect ourselves from our own timeline in order not to remember them. And when our future promises, because of expectations based in past experience, to burden us with still more pain we've already found unendurable (cf. Winnicott, 1974), we try to bring time itself to a standstill (Schmithüsen, 2013) in order to halt its progress towards inevitable catastrophe.

How, though, do we effect this arrest of the inevitable movement of time? In his paper on the phenomenon of time at a "standstill" in the negative therapeutic reaction, Schmithüsen observes that, in psycho-analytic literature, "there seems to be an agreement on the brief state of timelessness in the experience of the newborn infant", and cites Loewald as having described the infantile state "as one without desire, memory, or anticipation. There is no separation between past, present, and future, only the experience of an inseparable mother–child unit free from tension or desire" (2013, p. 72). From this, we might conclude that the retreat to timelessness can be regarded as a fantasied regression to an early infantile state, in much the same spirit as that described by Grunberger and Chasseguet-Smirgel. To Chasseguet-Smirgel's assertion that the fantasy of the smooth maternal belly functions to avoid the reality of the father, his penis, and other children, we would only add that time itself is a part of the reality that becomes intolerable for some patients, and that atemp-orality is an essential, if sometimes overlooked, subtext of the dream of the return to the womb.

To live within time means we have submitted to the painful realities of the world—death, loss, disappointment—and have found ways to make those realities tolerable. To attempt to live without time—to seek the timelessness of resting in the arms of the god-object—means that time itself has become synonymous with trauma, and we have committed ourselves to avoiding it—even if it requires doing violence to our capacity to live in the human world. The timeless patient hates living in time, hates the events that occur in time, and consequently, tries to sever all ties that would connect him to it.

In a session in the first year of treatment, Doug told me, in a very matter-of-fact tone, of a dream he'd had the night before. In the dream, he watched a video of himself sleeping. He knew, in this dream, that the Doug on the video was dreaming, and that the dream was of his childhood abuse. With this dream, Doug took *two* radical steps away from his temporal connectedness, both with himself and with me. First, the version of himself that dreamt of past abuse was not the actual Doug; it was instead a version that had been turned into a *mere object* of Doug's perception—a transformation that had distanced that version, and the trauma it contained, from the moment-to-moment contents of the actual Doug's mind. Second, he told me of this dream with such an emotional disconnectedness that it was clear he expected me only to be entertained by it, and not to want to *do* anything with it, such as use it to uncover more about Doug's trauma or help him work through its long-term effects (both activities, of course, would have taken place in the nexus of past, present, and future). When I suggested to Doug that the dream symbolised a self-protective detachment both from his abuse and from the work we were attempting to accomplish, he responded with a profound lack of interest, as though he had retreated to a state of suspended animation from which all investment in the past (his abuse), the present (his interaction with me), or the future (the possibility of working through) had been evacuated.

The means by which Doug achieved this state of timelessness was, of course, his elimination of emotion and his unconscious embrace of the god-object. Because Doug's past was full of trauma and his future promised more of the same, and because his anger with those who have been, or might be, instrumental in causing him pain remained unacknowledged, the most effective way of avoiding future pain and punishing his persecutors was to separate himself from those emotions and psychic states that would bind him to them. And the most effective way of accomplishing this was to embrace the god-object (that internal "delusional object" that offers the promise of "complete painlessness"—Rosenfeld, 1971, p. 175) and the fantasy it provides of re-entering the safety of the womb. By activating this fantasy, Doug established an internal state in which he lived without worry or direction for the future, without anxiety that in his present he might be injured or injure another, and without acknowledgement that his past, in the form of fear, hate, and other relationship-relevant emotions, continues to agitate the depths of his unconscious.

As with many patients in a traumatic retreat, Doug's timelessness was even more visible in the broader patterns of his life. For most of his life, Doug displayed what can only be called an unremitting penchant for non-activity. Not only did he avoid working through his past traumas; he also avoided undertaking any of the possible activities that might lift him out of the greyness that pervaded his life. Despite his steady attendance in therapy, he did not alter his daily routines: he still watched movies, he still skied and played pool, he still dated without planning for a future, and although he talked of starting a career, he persistently made no move towards that end. It wasn't that he actively or consciously resisted changing; it was more that it didn't *occur* to him that change was something to aim for. Because of his wholesale ejection of his emotional life, and because he had unlinked past, present, and future, any thought or desire he might have had to create a different way of being in the future was unconsciously negated and consigned to the categories of "never-thought" and "never-felt".

Doug's case, which is far from unique, is reminiscent of patients described by many authors. Civitarese, for example, reported a case in which he thought he was working with the "autistic areas of the mind": "Here," he said, "everything that occurs is characterised by negativity: 'Nothing' seems to be happening. ... Time never passes. It stops, melts away like the clock in Dali's famous painting" (2016b, p. 12). Similarly, Davoine and Gaudillière describe cases of traumatised patients in which "[n]othing changes, nothing has changed, nothing can change. It's always the same thing, no progress. ... [The analyst] suddenly sees that, where he is now with this patient, time is no longer functioning as it did before" (2004, pp. 177–178). And Green (1975) spoke of a patient who sought to "attain a state of emptiness and aspires to non-being and nothingness" (p. 7). In this case, Green says, the analyst "feels caught in the patient's network of mummified objects, paralysed in his activity and unable to stimulate any curiosity in the patient about himself" (pp. 5–6).

I did indeed feel caught in the network of Doug's "mummified objects"—to the extent that his commitment to non-activity gave me a feeling that I was bound up, like a mummy, and that I could not move because I had no direction and because I was not really a full object for him anyway, and any movement I attempted was negated by his aggressive detachment and embrace of timelessness. I was frustrated by this, because at the same time I felt paralysed I also believed his very presence in therapy constituted a *request*—for me to do his thinking for him and to give him, as a gift, a way to come back to life out of his nothingness. Because Doug was unable to bring his emotions to our sessions on his own, I felt that I was the one who held his emotions, in my mind, for him. And because I did, I often also had the feeling that I was persecuting him with them. Whenever I introduced them in our conversation, I felt vaguely cruel, as though I was either making him swallow medicine he hated and was convinced would injure him, or I was causing him fresh pain, of the very sort that led him into his retreat in the first place. When working with timeless patients, even the gentlest of therapeutic strategies feel to them like a fresh injury, because therapy, with its focus on change and development, represents a world they have long tried to escape.

I have suggested that a primary motivation for patients' embrace of the god-object and retreat into timelessness is the opportunity it affords them to enact aggression without having to acknowledge or take responsibility for it. That aggression can be seen in the countertransference reactions I've just described. The frustration I felt when working with Doug was directly linked to the fact that working with him placed me in an "impossible" situation: he asked me to help him while, at the same time, refusing or negating my attempts to do so. It was as though he was saying to me, or to his mother, or his abuser, or even his absent father: "I am so angry with you that I will forever taunt you with the possibility that you can gain access to me, but I will structure my mind so that it will never, ever happen." In Doug's case, and in many cases like Doug's, this aggression is central to the patient's overall functioning, and their improvement depends on the therapist helping them detoxify it—along with the pain with which it is intertwined—and thereby hold it in their minds, in their self-identities, as an accepted and acknowledged part of themselves.

The seductive allure of desire

I selected the title for this segment because it captures an ambiguity about *who* it is that is seduced when a patient seeks to bring time to a standstill. Clearly, the patients I am describing are seduced by the promise that they can escape pain by retreating to the god-object and the timelessness it offers. But in this section, I'd like to focus on the seductive allure that the *therapist* feels when working with such patients. That allure has the potential, more so than with many other patients, to draw the therapist into substantial alterations in technique, to try to reach the patient who has retreated from the working relationship.

Psychoanalytic literature is full of descriptions of the strong counter-transference reactions therapists experience when working with these patients. Possible reactions include sadism (Asch, 1976), body tension (Pontalis, 2014), masochism (Finell, 1987), inaction and a "throttling" of the analytic process (Baranger, 1974), and feelings of guilt and helplessness (Cohen, 1993). When such reactions are present, they create a strain on the therapist's analytic neutrality (Sandler, Dare & Holder, 1973/1992) and an escalation of what Cohen would have called the clinician's "therapeutic zeal" (Cohen, 1993, p. 124; see also Wurmser & Jarass, 2013b), leading the therapist to try to "sell" the idea of progress to the patient, and to either coax the patient towards that progress, or force him towards it with manic or retaliatory acts (cf. Welles & Wrye, 1991). For a therapist to succumb to this temptation is tantamount to transforming the patient into an object of manipulation, a failure of therapeutic technique that is akin to what

Davoine and Gaudillière have described as an "illusion of possible mastery" (2004, p. 168)—a defensive belief that a timely and well-formed intervention can bring a patient rapidly, and almost magically, out of trauma and into psychological health.

Although these countertransference reactions may originate in unresolved conflicts within the therapist alone, their more common origin lies in the therapist's introjective identification (Scharff, 1992) with split-off and projected contents of the patient's unconscious. Gabbard has noted that it is widely accepted that the therapist's countertransference "may reflect the patient's attempt to evoke feelings in the analyst that the patient cannot tolerate" (Gabbard, 1996, p. 70), and Grotstein has offered an eloquent description of the process:

> I believe that one can alternatively regard the psychoanalytic process ... as one in which some inner function within the patient that senses his difficulty but has no words for it unconsciously recruits the analyst to play a complementary role so that a play or dramatic *en-act*-ment can take place. It is like playing serious charades where the patient signals the experience of his demon in such a dramatic way that the analyst can interpret it. In the meanwhile, however, the analyst is unconsciously drawn into the play so that the purposeful drama can take place. (2009, p. 218)

Patients in retreat to the god-object are highly prone to mobilise sequences of projective and introjective identification in the therapeutic relationship because their traumatic history has given them powerful internal motivations to split off, refuse to acknowledge, or fail to represent the parts of themselves their condemnatory superego finds objectionable.

We noted earlier that patients who embrace the god-object are suffering from a fundamental split in their psyches, between the demonic superego that shames them and the god-object that guarantees their righteous goodness at the cost of abandoning objectionable emotions and desires. The pivotal implication of this internal system is that these patients *do* experience desires and emotions that their superego finds condemnable, and that this is the case even when these patients *appear* to have emptied themselves of offending internal content. This fact deserves emphasis for two reasons. First, it isn't uncommon for authors who write about these kinds of patients to focus too predominantly on the *negating* side of the patients' dilemma—that is, on the part of the patient that seeks to eliminate objectionable emotions/desires. This has contributed to the bias that can be found in analytic discussions, and which seems to be embedded in the term "negative therapeutic reaction", that these patients are devoted, almost exclusively, to undermining therapeutic progress. The fact that they may unconsciously *want* to improve, or to emerge from their retreat to experience emotion more fully, or to engage with others in terms of desire, sexual or otherwise, is too often overlooked. Pontalis, for example, suggested that, at base, these patients "are asking us to *cure them of sexuality*, an ineducable, incurable sexuality which is for them … charged with hatred, envy and violence. Rather than measure up to the madness of Eros, they choose the lost cause of a battle with Thanatos" (1980, p. 28, original emphasis), and Chasseguet-Smirgel has said that these patients attempt to reproduce in the relationship with the analyst "the fantasied destruction of both partners in the primal scene" because they are fundamentally motivated by

> the hatred of life, the non-acceptance of the primal scene as liable to give birth to a child, and, consequently the impossibility of forming a couple with the analyst so as to give birth to a child that would be themselves. (1985a, p. 112, p. 116)

Although neither Pontalis nor Chasseguet-Smirgel are inaccurate in pointing to such aspects of these patients, the issue is one of emphasis and completeness: to overemphasise patients' motives for self-negation is to underestimate the full parameters of the dilemma they face.

Second, if these patients' repressed emotions and desires are ignored, then a key reason for the very existence of their internal psychic system is also overlooked. Patients in retreat to a god-object do not seek treatment because they have *succeeded* in eliminating their objectionable emotions/ desires, or even because they unambiguously *wish* to, but because they are paralysed by an impossible choice between a superego that condemns them for having those feelings and a god-object that presents itself as the only source of safety, but at the cost of repressing or evacuating everything that brings them to life. The existence of such a dilemma accounts for the fact that clinicians, when working with these patients, are more prone than usual to "*en-act*" (in Grotstein's terms), through their countertransference, the unacceptable parts of the patient's mind. The dilemma also helps to explain why patients diligently attend treatment, even while they actively, if unconsciously, impede its progress.

Although therapists experience many kinds of countertransference reactions with patients in retreat, I would like to focus in this section on one kind of reaction—that arising from the therapist's identification with the patient's desire. We've already seen an example, in my work with Doug, of a patient's repressed and projected desire generating disturbing countertransference emotions. My feeling that I was persecuting Doug by raising his shame or anger as topics of conversation indicated that *I*, not he, almost exclusively possessed and acknowledged the desire that he benefit from treatment. My ownership of this desire was, in large part, a result of my identification with the hidden part of Doug that *did* want to improve. Following Bion and Rosenfeld, I thought of this as the sane or healthy part of Doug's personality, because it was this part that brought him to therapy and kept him there. The problem, of course, was that Doug's desire for improvement was inconsistent with his defence of seeking timelessness and the god-object as guarantors of security and camouflage for aggression. (It is important to note that by my identifying with Doug's desire, he and I reached a type of communion, in which together we represented the totality of his mind and experience, and through which the possibility arose of recognising that his need to embrace the god-object coexisted with his desire to leave it.)

Experiencing a countertransference resonance with a patient's repressed desire to improve is not, however, the only form of desire that can appear in the therapist in interactions with these patients. There are other forms of desire that should be considered as well, and in what follows I will examine a few of the more prominent forms. To do so, I will introduce two additional patients, each of whom elicited differing countertransference reactions (but each revolving around desire) in the therapist.

Harold, an effeminate young man raised by self-absorbed parents who set rigid, limiting expectations and punished him with moralistic condemnations (based in religious beliefs) when he didn't meet them, developed a conviction that his real emotions were worthy of irremediable condemnation. To avoid the dangers of these condemnations, he (like Doug) stifled self-expression in order to achieve a calm, unprovocative relationship with his parents and an internal union with a god-object that granted him righteous goodness as long as he did nothing to trigger additional condemnations. In many of our sessions, Harold was personable but unreachable: he exhibited no pressing need to change and he was eerily content with how his internal and external worlds were structured. He once acknowledged, with an air of self-satisfaction, that he had constructed his mind so that nothing I could say would move him "even an inch" from where he was comfortable, and he saw no reason to change that arrangement. As this exchange between us was repeated, multiple times, over the next few months, I came to see him as almost being asleep, resting in an eternal slumber, inanimate and insouciant, and uninvited by internal or external urges. It was at this point that I began to feel that I wanted to break into his chamber, to "wake" him from his somnolence and bring him back into reality, towards growth and interaction, and his own desire. I recognised this was my countertransference and that its origin lay in Harold's projections, but the feeling nonetheless was potent. My desire seemed to me to be akin to what the handsome prince might have felt as he was seeking Sleeping Beauty to awaken her with a kiss.

Lou was raised in a family that included a sister who was later diagnosed as borderline psychotic, a demanding mother who rarely expressed love, and a father prone to unexpected attacks over minor offences, Lou developed a psychic structure marked by paranoia and aggressive devaluation of others, but also extreme anxiety—both about harming others with his aggression as well as disappointing them with his "failures" in his performance (at whatever task) and subsequently drawing their criticisms. Lou defended against this anxiety with procrastination, a sense of entitlement, and a "timeless" approach to his life in which he felt no urgency to change. When I once observed to him that he regularly discounted my interpretations, he said interpretations felt to him like I was attempting to "penetrate him from behind". A repeating occurrence in our sessions has been for Lou to state that he wasn't changing because of flaws in my technique and my "psychoanalytic assumptions", and to suggest that he would be better off seeing a cognitive behavioural therapist who would give him the correct assignments to make him change. I interpreted these moments as revealing Lou's fear of owning the desire to change on his own, and his anger with me for refusing to own that desire myself, but as these interactions recurred I grew frustrated with my inability to reach him or to mobilise his curiosity as to why he was in such a paralysed position. At this point I began to contemplate either referring him to a cognitive behavioural therapist or changing my technique to provide cognitive behavioural treatment to Lou myself.

The first thing to notice in the cases of both Harold and Lou is that I felt excluded from their inner worlds and unable to reach them. At first glance these feelings might appear to be an ordinary, unremarkable consequence of working with a patient in retreat, but in actuality they represent an identification with some of the more regressive aspects of the patients' unconscious. Remember that Chasseguet-Smirgel has argued that these patients are motivated by a fantasy that they can *return* to the smooth maternal belly, having already experienced envy of the other occupants of that belly (father's phallus, other siblings). Grotstein has offered a vivid description of this kind of envy:

> Mother's interiority is infancy's castle and cathedral. It is the domain of the sacred that the infant idealises but also seeks to profane—out of envy, which is Klein's (1928) view. I hypothesise that the envy that this 'infantile raider of the lost ark' experiences … is one of feelings of injustice, rivalry, desire for revenge, and demand to be restored to their lost kingdom: omnipotence. It is as if the infant is saying, "Mother's body was once *my* home, and I have been unceremoniously evicted from it. … Every time I gaze at mother's body, particularly her breasts, I cannot help remembering that they were once mine and *she* was once *me*, and now I find myself on the outside gazing at her and them longingly …" (2009, p. 219)

It shouldn't escape our notice that the feelings of exclusion Grotstein and Chasseguet-Smirgel attribute to the infant are quite similar to what I experienced with Harold and Lou. If we think of my feelings as not merely a reaction to these patients being in retreat, but an introjective identification with repressed desires, then we will have discovered a foundational emotional conflict that helps push these patients towards their god-objects. That is, my desire to reach them in their retreats was motivated, at least in part, by my countertransferential identification with their envy of the womb and the longing to return to it. As Grotstein suggested, these patients need the therapist to "*en-act*" their most unthinkable pain: by retreating to their inner sanctum and excluding their therapists, they induce in therapists the same envy and anxiety they (the patients) felt when *they* were excluded, as well as the same longing to return to the womb's timeless safety.

This regressive identification, on the part of the therapist, with a patient's desire to return to the womb, can appear in another form as well—in the therapist's attempt to *become* the womb for the patient and to thereby "perpetuate excessively a mother–baby fusion" (Welles & Wrye, 1991, p. 95). The fact that the therapist here may be playing the role of the mother who *provides* the womb, and not of the infant who has *retreated into* it, matters little in terms of the potential gratifications to be gained and the anxieties to be avoided.

Therapists may experience still other desires, besides those revolving around envy, when working with patients in traumatic retreat. Reflecting the patient's essential ambivalence about the value or necessity of the womb, the therapist may, at the same time she feels envy, also be induced to want to reach into the womb and rescue the infant from his peaceful but spiritless slumber. In this case, the therapist's countertransference reflects the part of the patient that wants the mother or father (or the mother/father dyad that protects the mother from being colonised by the infant frightened of the external world) to help the patient escape his retreat, or at least to help smooth the way, to offer a hybrid form of being in which he can get a taste of object-instinctual living, while at the same time retaining his reassuring connection with the womb. In my image of Harold as a Sleeping Beauty whom I, as a Prince, would awaken with a kiss, the kiss may well symbolise this hybrid form of rescue. On the one hand, it represents the discrete action that would bring Harold back into the world. But on the other, it evokes a mother's kiss on the lips, a deeply unconscious reminder, as Grunberger has suggested, of the "liquid environment" of the womb, and of the "substance in which the foetus splashes around" (1989, p. 68).

Paul Auster's novel, *Mr. Vertigo*, is about a character, Walt, who learns as a child to levitate. His ability to fly, in which he rejoices, not only rescues him from his abusive and traumatic upbringing, but it also makes him famous. As he approaches adolescence, however, it begins to make him dangerously ill. He rejects the only cure, castration, and spends the rest of his life firmly rooted to the ground. Near the end, though, Walt wonders if he should teach anyone else to fly. It would be easy, he tells the reader: You must only "learn to stop being yourself", "let yourself evaporate", and "breathe until you feel your soul pouring out of you" (1994, pp. 293–294).

It is possible to interpret Walt's flying as akin to a retreat to a god-object. Patients who utilise this kind of retreat face an impossible choice of whether to stay with a defence that has protected them, and even given them pleasure, but that has also hampered their ability to be enlivened, embodied, and "personalised", in Winnicott's sense (1962, p. 59) of feeling that their bodies are appropriate loci of desire and initiative. When the therapist feels the desire to coax such a patient out of this retreat, the therapist is enacting part of the drama of the patient's life that the patient cannot himself express, and is taking on the role Joyce McDougall assigns to the young mother, whose maternal function "must include her desire to seduce her baby to want to live" (1982, p. 382). By doing so, the therapist enacts the patient's deeply repressed desire for the mother to do her job to make the world safe enough for him to emerge.

Another form of desire that is visible in the above vignettes, particularly Lou's, has a less maternal and more aggressive tonality. Whereas the maternal desire is to coax the infant/patient to emerge from his retreat, the aggressive or paternal form is to force that emergence with an act of authority. The oedipal aspect of this form of desire is evident in the patient's corresponding transference, which communicates to the therapist something like, "I'm paralysed here in the inner sanctum and I need someone from the outside to extract me from my mother's womb." The therapist's desire in this case represents the hidden part of the patient who wants the father to recognise the necessity of breaking up the fused child–mother dyad and to both reclaim his wife and liberate the child. With Lou, this desire appeared in my considering the possibility of referring him to CBT, which in my countertransference I regarded as a system of authoritative demands, while Lou expressed his fear of the intruding father (a fear that coexisted with a desire for the intrusion—recall Freud's claim that behind every fear is a wish) through such images as my "penetrating him from behind" with my interpretations. This particular configuration of the therapeutic relationship is more likely to appear when patients were infantilised by mother, or trapped in mother's erotised need for her child's symbiotic attachment.

Clearly, we can frame the therapist's countertransference desires in terms of the patient's transferences. The transference that says, "I hate you for not making my entry into the world safe, so you must keep out and long for me forever", corresponds to the therapist's envy and longing to join the patient in the womb—either as a twin or as the womb itself; and the transference saying "Please enter my inner sanctum and rescue me" mobilises the therapist's desire to become the mother who coaxes, or the father who demands, the child's separation from the womb. The final transference–countertransference profile we will consider is based in the patient's unacknowledged desire to enter, or *begin* to enter, the world of mature sexual relationships, either by actively seducing the therapist or passively becoming the object of the therapist's desire. Typically, this kind of desire is linked to the oedipal complex, when the child is beginning to explore sexual longings and sexual jealousies (Grotstein, 2009). Because patients who retreat to the god-object faced, in general, massive pressures to repress unacceptable impulses at the time of Oedipus, the appearance of their unconscious erotic longings in treatment carry with them many of the characteristics of the oedipal phase, including gender confusion and a mixture of homoerotic and heteroerotic desires (Freud, 1923b; McDougall, 1995). When therapists identify with these unconscious longings, they will tend to have fantasies or dream images that contain similar characteristics. Hence, while my Sleeping Beauty image represented, from one perspective, Harold's desire to be awakened from his womb-like slumber, from another it captured his desire to explore sexuality, undifferentiated as it may have been at the time it was repressed, in a context free of the condemnations of his demonic superego (the old witch of the fairy tale?). Similarly, Lou's image of my interpretations penetrating him from behind, as well as my fantasy of overpowering his resistances with CBT, reflect not only his desire to be rescued from his retreat, but also the emergence of undifferentiated oedipo-erotic desires, this time in a more aggressive form.

To conclude this section: it is always worth reminding ourselves that because of the intimate connections between one person's unconscious and another's, our patients always have at hand the means to communicate to us psychic states of which they have no conscious awareness. The analysis of the desires the therapist experiences, particularly when working with patients in a traumatic retreat to the god-object, helps us to both understand more fully the etiology and internal dynamics of their defences, and, being more attuned to the patients' hidden dimensions, approach them with an attitude and array of techniques that more effectively helps them reclaim the lost parts of their personalities.

Conclusion

While there are many other important characteristics of patients who have retreated to the god-object (including, for example: their sacrifice of themselves or others to appease their superego; their preference for regressive suffering rather than mourning; their devotion to rescuing or healing the internal mother rather than separating from her; their perfectionism and tendency to control internal and external environments; their reliance on magical thinking; and their aggression and envy that contributed to the formation of their defences in the first place), many of which are investigated by the other authors in this book, the characteristics we have considered in this chapter—the nature of the god-object, the allure of timelessness, the transfer of desire from patient to therapist, and the etiology of these defences in traumatic family experiences—are pivotal in helping the therapist understand these patients and determining whether and how to treat them. These patients embody one of the most profound paradoxes in all psychopathology, in that while they long to be helped, they are also masters at throwing roadblocks in the path of treatment. To work with them is to submit oneself to frustration and an endless variety of countertransference perturbations, but it also exposes the therapist to the depths of human suffering and to the moving possibilities of healing and redemption.

CHAPTER FIVE

Clinical factors in the treatment of the traumatised, resistant patient

Charles Ashbach, Karen Fraley, Paul Koehler, and James Poulton

Summary statement

To briefly reprise the thesis of this book: The individual we are seeking to understand suffers from a condition of chronic resistance and inaccessibility resulting from the trauma of having lost attachment and sustaining emotional contact with the primal figure of the mother of childhood. Of course other forms of trauma exist but in seeking to understand the problems of this patient we focus on the issue of what Green (1986) terms the "dead mother" complex. Here, the mother has suffered a catastrophic loss of her own primary figure (parent, spouse, sibling, or child) that has led to her preoccupation in a state of bereavement producing an indifference and unavailability to the figures of need and attachment in her world. The abandoned child of this mother experiences a denial or exclusion from access to the "soul and spirit" of the mother and as a result suffers a painful collapse of central elements of his personality.

Freud in "Mourning and melancholia" (1917e) tells us that the subject in such a situation seeks to re-establish the "lost" love object through identification and establish it within the unconscious aspect of the ego to protect against the unbearable, chaotic experience of radical abandonment. Ogden (2002, p. 771) points out how the self is "poor and empty" (narcissistically depleted) without the experience of the object and suffers from the burden of being tormented by self-condemnation on the one side and self-righteous outrage on the other. In the face of such a danger the subject reconstructs his psychic world by creating a series of compensating replacement objects that allow for some measure of stability in dealing with the storms of love and hate resulting from the loss.

This reconstructed inner world is built around three central figures: first, an ideal object of beauty, power, and perfection drawn from memories and omnipotent fantasies that offers the subject the delusion of possessing the figure of perfect security and love; second, an internal bad object formed to contain the anger, violence, and fury associated with the loss and injustice of his situation; and third, the figure of the "damaged" object of love and need is established at the core of the self where the subject feels compelled to repair and restore it to an imagined position of grandeur and perfection in order for him to feel complete, loved, and secure. The subject unconsciously feels a sense of "primary omnipotent responsibility" (Wurmser, 2007, p. 34) for the "damage" done to the object and is driven by a powerful sense of guilt and shame—Klein's (1935) depressive position—to work unceasingly till the object's reparation or restoration is successful. Riviere (1936) observes that the subject's guilt concerning the fate of the primary object is a central point of resistance because the patient will not allow himself to benefit from the therapy if the object (the internal form of the external object) continues to exist in its compromised and injured state.

The patient radically splits his personality as he experiences the double bind of feeling both absolutely guilty for his loss and completely innocent for a circumstance that has befallen him. He is now a house divided, suffering from a double consciousness (Wurmser, 2007) and facing the impossible tormenting challenge of reconciling these extreme states of psychic and emotional contradiction between his guilt and his innocence. And always, lurking in the depth of his unconscious is the damaged primary internal object that demands his attention and the resolution of its injury.

The violence and shock of his loss has corrupted the subject's superego, endowing it with a primitive edge of judgement and moral condemnation. The subject seeks to manage the bifurcation of his core-self by establishing a false self (Winnicott, 1960) mask that allows him to appear present, congenial, and cooperative, all the while troubled by the question: is he good or bad? The patient sets out to control the therapist and the treatment in order to obtain a narcissistic measure of comfort and power without risking exposure, vulnerability, and the dangers of intimacy. Accordingly, with this intricate defence system the treatment is not allowed to penetrate to the depth of the subject's personality as he keeps more primitive paranoid–schizoid dimensions (Klein, 1946) hidden from the working-through process. The result is a treatment that is both shallow and tenacious with a sense of dead-ended repetition and narrowness that leads the therapist into a feeling of hopelessness, impotence, and frustration.

The patient is likewise frustrated and confused because he is unable to learn from experience (Bion, 1962) and, as importantly, is unable to accomplish the miracle of reversing the loss and thereby resolving the inner torment of his abandoned self. The subject unconsciously seeks to magically restore the primary object that is the true but secret goal powering the subject's participation in the treatment. Faced with these failures the subject regresses to the depth of his unconscious and constructs what Freud termed a "private religion" (1907b, p. 119) out of the rituals, obsessive practices, and ceremonies of the treatment. This regression seeks to provide the subject with the power of a supernatural figure, a god-object that might be petitioned for help and relief. The crucial element in this religious gambit is the activation of the delusion of omnipotent power (Novick & Novick, 1991, p. 310) through an omnipotent masochistic fantasy where "everything painful is turned into a sign of special favor, uniqueness and magical power (Novick & Novick, 1991, p. 315).

The subject's belief is founded upon the activation of a manic, omnipotent fantasy where his loss and suffering are considered signs leading, inevitably, to the power to be able to shape his life and take control of significant figures within it. He unconsciously denies the tragedy of his losses and seeks the magical power he associates with his perverse experience of violence and the destruction of the good and valuable in his life. Thus, an unconscious process of sacrificial destruction is developed where the subject offers up the most valuable elements of his life, his work, and relationships in order to secure the proper relationship with his personal, self-created deity, that is, his ideal object. His sacrificial suffering serves to cover over his guilt and shame for attacking or destroying the good objects of his world.

Thus, what looks like "mere" resistance needs to be understood as a boundary condition that allows for the appearance of cooperation from the outside of the self while from the subjective side of the patient we see a world that is organised against the process of change and organised around the regressive desire to re-find the primary objects and re-establish the lost world of innocence, reconciliation, and invulnerability. In this "sacred" mode the therapy is felt to be the search for a supernatural (omnipotent) power that will end the subject's pain, guilt, and misery.

The psychological essence at the core of the actual treatment involves the subject taking the incredible risk of dependency and vulnerability as well as allowing himself to experience the pain and tragedies of his life that will lead to mourning and the genuine re-ordering of his life. Part and parcel of the patient's "religious" therapeutic process is his use of the therapist as a scapegoat figure (Girard, 1977) to bear the burdens of his guilt, shame, and crimes. The patient adopts the role of moral authority ("You should") and purity, reflecting the role of the objects in his childhood and seeks to punish and condemn the therapist as the replacement figure for the offending parental object of his childhood. Likewise, the patient's ability to stop the forward flow of the treatment is imagined to keep the "door to the past" open until such time that the trauma and loss of his childhood can be magically undone and a "new past" is created. The transference atmosphere in the sessions is filled with disagreement, antagonism, and frustration as the cover for the psychotic nature of the subject's experience of an imminent breakdown.

All of these manoeuvres are created to stop the movement of the treatment that seeks to engage the subject in a process of insight, feeling, grief, and mourning. The metabolisation of the ideal object at the core allows the patient to find a true and alive relationship with the therapist if he is able to bear the pain of recognising and understanding the particular and specific factors that made his life what it is. Such understanding unlocks the lost gratitude he feels for the gift of life, and even the trauma and deficits of his suffering are understood with an observer's more objective and empathetic view. The increased meaning and pleasure of the treatment unlocks the hidden libido that the subject refused to experience and begins to reduce the narcissistic pleasure of his omnipotent retreat. The treatment that had been made to be a sterile process now becomes alive with the possibility of new life, a new self for the patient.

The containment demands made on the therapist often overwhelm her ability to remain symbolic and to use the countertransference for clues to the unconscious agenda and dynamics active in the patient. The subject's weak ego boundaries lead to the interpenetration of the patient into the psyche of the therapist, thus producing intense states of confusion and *folie à deux*. The patient is terrified of closeness and paradoxically seeks the impossible intimacy of complete fusion. The lack of adequate separation prevents true symbolic communication from occurring with a feeling of breakdown and "stuckness". The challenge for the therapist is to survive these moments and phases of deep confusion in order to regain her symbolic capacity so that she may come out of her "trance" and think again, that is to become once again the therapist.

The arc of the treatment should move from the imprisonment of both the patient and the therapist in a timeless frozen moment to a position of mourning and aliveness where a new order of understanding offers the subject the possibility of insight, development, and growth. The following elements highlight some of the most important factors to consider in the work with the patient that seems unable or unwilling to use the therapy to separate from fantasised objects in order to find his way into the realm of reality, pleasure, pain, and limitation.

Resistance as a boundary condition

This understanding of resistance places it as a point of meaning reflecting psychic and emotional catastrophe. The subject seeks to stop time itself so that the treatment is prevented from uncovering the elements that will reactivate the trauma of his loss and the guilt and shame he experiences about his situation. The challenge for the therapist is to find the core experience that the patient protects and to construct a stance or position that will enable her to contain the patient's anxieties, to whatever point possible but to remain separate enough so that the strength of her symbolic understanding will be able to resist the violence and terror directed at the treatment. Psychotic and delusional elements are co-mingled in the transference and countertransference along with more mature and sophisticated psychic aspects presenting a changing and shifting diagnostic picture.

The existential threat to the subject's sense of self

In spite of the surface elements, the patient experiences his psychic experience to be in a fragile state and thus his ability to resist and be negative is felt to be a "personal asset" (Pontalis, 2014, p. 534). The ability to say "No!" without speaking, that is, through his behaviour and mad inaccessibility provides him with the experience of power and triumph. The patient manifests a "psychic anorexia" and the therapist is often trapped in her desire to feed and nurture the patient. As one patient described it:

"That thing you want me to give up (his opposition) is my spine." The patient as oppositional agent is now visible to the therapist and radically different from the mad, invisible, and insignificant figure of his childhood.

The "sacred" world of the traumatised patient

The psychic world created by the traumatised patient is outside the normal boundaries of space, time, and causality that we associate with the realm of reality testing. He seems present to us in the treatment but he is actually located in a different "register" of experience that is characterised by its phantasmic, wishful, and narcissistic qualities. He wants our help in accomplishing his impossible goals and the therapist needs to locate the exact nature of the patient's therapeutic ambition. At the core of his unconscious within his "private religion" he operates in a "sacred" world of wish, ritual, and magic omnipotence where the power of suffering is felt to be the decisive agent of change and transformation. An unconscious experience of sacrifice, the ceremonial destruction of something of value and worth is the bridge that the patient feels connects the moral subject to the divine object. In the patient's phantasy the god-object is the imagined source of power that provides the exclusive means of ending the subject's unbearable problems of loss, pain, guilt, and abandonment, producing the glorious realisation of his dreams.

On the use of the therapist by the patient

The patient uses aspects of himself and the therapist as sacrificial scapegoats that may be systematically destroyed so the ideal part of the self may be allowed to live on. He seeks a condition of purity and perfection and the use of his violence shows the importance of his search. Sin or badness as well as madness and dread must be projected into "other" (both in the self and in the therapist) so that he can hope to remain protected from the dangers of human vulnerability and frailty. He believes the magic of suffering and sacrifice will enable him to transform "suffering into pleasure, anxiety into sexual excitement, hatred into love, separation into fusion, helplessness into power and revenge, guilt into forgiveness and shame into triumph ..." (Wurmser, 2007, p. 268). Instead of the healthy triad of guilt, mourning, and reparation that is the product of a successful separation, the patient believes, with a religious conviction, that the magical power of the sacrificial process of pain and suffering achieves the manic triad of what Freud defined as "joy, exultation and triumph" (1917e, p. 254). A preference for hate and sadism suggests such patients often develop a perverse attitude towards the treatment and therapist.

The body, suffering, and symbolism

This patient, unable to learn from experience continues to operate in an emotionally non-symbolic, concretistic mode (Segal, 1957) where he "feels" the pains in his body and mind but cannot make sense of or use them to find meaning. Here we become aware of the subject's inability to engage in the progressive action of psychic suffering where pain, when processed through the body experience allows for deeper connections to unconscious meanings and their significance. The patient feels emotional pain but can derive no meaning and significance within it. It is this dissociated bodily reaction that must be engaged if the therapist is to help the patient liberate the frozen, traumatic memories that block the connection to the core of the self and thus exclude the forward movement of the treatment. Hidden within the beta, body states (Bion, 1962) is the fear of psychotic breakdown and psychic fragmentation that marks the great danger of patient's connection to his emotional experiences.

On the agony of relinquishing the ideal object

The internal objects involved in traumatic loss are woven within the tissues of the subject's body (beta states) and thus the process of giving them up, both the missing actual object and the pathological fetish object, releases an enormous amount of emotional (cathartic reaction) suffering. One patient said that the "agony" of coming to terms with this situation seems too much to endure but it seemed he had no other choice. The process demands a great deal of empathy and sympathy on the part of the therapist as well as the humility of experiencing similar feelings to the patient about his need to metabolise his impossibly addictive dreams and longings. The slow process of connection and integration achieves progress not by a focus on the future or on any specific behavioural factor or accomplishment, rather by the descent into the fibre of the subject's being where life might be activated once again. As one patient said: "This is a new birth for me".

On the primitive nature of the transference

The transference, and thus the countertransference, acquire a dimensionality and particular aliveness where projections on to the surface of the therapist become the "invasion" into the substance of his character. As Davoine and Gaudillière (2004) point out the traumatized is unable to speak authentically and subjectively and must therefore "inscribe" his true meanings, through enactments and projective identifications into the being of the therapist, there to be recovered through the reflection and introspection of the countertransference and given back to the patient for his consideration. Here the therapist acts as "agent" for the patient, not sharing his autobiography but offering the patient the evidence of her recovery of the dissociated aspects of the subject's experience through the therapist's intuitive and emotional reverie.

Mourning and the grieving of lost infantile experiences

The patient seeks to deny his problems of failed attachment and seeks to eradicate the barriers of time, sexual, and generational differences as well as the difference between reality and fantasy. He seeks through seduction, manipulation, and aggression to enforce his unique and fantastic world on to/into the therapist. With the destruction of boundaries, the loss of the primary object can be denied and the ideal object, though imagined, thin, and illusory may be clung to as the available replacement for the actual external figure of the parental object(s). The obliteration of sexual boundaries offers the subject a hiding place so that he doesn't have to contend with the oedipal challenge, the solidification of the third, and the acceptance of sexual identity. The flight from genuine sexuality leads to a "sterile" form of treatment (Chasseguet-Smirgel, 1985a, p. 115) that stops the clinical partnership from producing the new birth of the patient's alive self.

On the limits of the therapeutic process

The therapist can better appreciate the limits of the therapeutic process if she is able to identify the delusional elements lurking at the core of both her and the patient's therapeutic goals, that is, the desire to magically repair the damaged, primary maternal object through the omnipotence ("religion") of the treatment (Racker, 1968). For some patients the best they can do is to "approximate" treatment and stay away from the powerfully disorganising reality of their traumatic childhood. They often seek treatment as an end-in-itself and are not interested in being "returned" to the world. When the therapist can better make a determination as to her goals in the treatment she will be better able to address the patient and his dreams and needs. The question of the therapist's masochism, sadism, and mania are to be considered in the question of whether to continue or terminate the treatment.

On the two therapeutic roles for the therapist

We see that at core there are two primary roles for the therapist to occupy in the working-through process of the treatment. On the regressive side is the therapist's role as the "sacrificial scapegoat" who seeks to help the patient by taking his burdens on as *her* problems. This regressive role is evidence of the confusion on the part of the therapist and the presence of unmetabolised guilt (masochism) that drives her to offer herself "up" to her own god-figure of power and forgiveness. On the progressive side is the role of the therapist as assisting the patient to be able to "live" (fully experience) the loss and tragedy of his early attachment failures and to be able to depend on the therapist as the "new" figure of attachment that might lead to actual mourning and real separation on his way to an authentic and meaningful existence. This role of the therapist as assistant, squire, and loyal partner is termed in antiquity as the "therapon" and is the basis for our word "therapist". In *Don Quixote* Sancho Panza is "therapon" to the Don as he seeks to help him to give up his delusions of impossible grandeur and glory and descend into the realm of loving husband and father who might be able to regain his status as the head of his household and resist the delusions of being the noble knight of chivalry who was to rescue the suffering damsels of his imagination, that is, the damaged internal object of the lost mother.

Clinical vignettes

We end this chapter with a series of clinical vignettes to illustrate the various forms in which unconscious elements emerge through "symbolic derivatives" (Ferro, 2005, p. 42). The transference and countertransference become the setting that allows for the externalization and representation of psychic–emotional objects buried in the unrememberable depths of the body–mind and the therapist is continually challenged to find a symbolic position, through intuition or "hallucinosis" (Bion, 1970, p. 36) to decode these vitally important proto-meanings and experiences. The goal is to use the inscribed traumatic elements to "achieve emotional unison with the patient" and thus to be able to be able to support the transformations that lead to understanding, repair and integration of the self (Ferro & Civitarese, 2015, p. 99).

On differentiating mourning from melancholia

Freud said that the dream is the "royal road" to the unconscious (1900) and the following vignette demonstrates the ways in which a central challenge in the personality can be represented through a dream. Here we are interested in the crisis of the lost object and the subject's defensive efforts to establish a connection with that object in the face of conflict and trauma.

Miss X and the dream of the bifurcated house

Miss X, a fifty-four-year-old, divorced, childless human resources manager who has been in once a week psychoanalytic psychotherapy for five years, reports a dream. She is standing in front of what appears to be her childhood home and sees to her amazement that it still has its freshly painted appearance, with a neat front lawn on a lovely street. As she gazes upon the scene she thinks she hears a baby crying and following the sound walks to the rear of the structure only to discover the back of the house collapsed and dilapidated and apparently has been that way for some time. She clearly hears a baby crying from within but does not dare enter the house for fear of the roof falling in on her. A woman standing in the yard next to her house says: "I hear a baby crying, don't you think you should see if she's alright?" Irritated at the woman for not offering help she returns to the front of the house. Once there she no longer hears the crying and walks away. She has reported this dream previously but this time she is agitated and disturbed by her seeming indifference.

Interpretative responses

Miss X's first association was to the run-down house as representing her mother who was born in a broken-down home in an impoverished, rural area. She feels a pang of guilt as she reports the dream and feels like she has abandoned a responsibility that absolutely belonged to her. She asks: "How could I be so callous and indifferent? Why didn't I at least call the police?" She was bothered by her response which seemed strange and then felt confused about not being able to determine what was real and what was imaginary about the sound of the crying child. She remembered thinking to herself: "If something is wrong then you should fix it." She emphasised the word "should" in her self-criticism.

Our discussion of the dream over a period of months opened up a cluster of three meanings. The first was about the mother-as-baby buried in the depression and poverty of her childhood. Miss X felt from an early age that she was tasked with the care of her mother who suffered a series of illnesses and depression and the phrase "parentified child" had long been in her mind.

Gradually as the dream became an element of the sessions she thought that a second meaning was that she was the crying baby and the seemingly unmotivated neighbour might represent her mother, who seemed unmoved by Miss X's plight. The mother's illnesses and depression often made her unable to attend to Miss X and her two younger siblings. Later, in response to the therapist's questioning, she said that perhaps this figure might include the therapist, who at times seems indifferent to her troubles and anxieties. She had not shared such transference thoughts before.

Subsequent discussions yielded a third meaning: Why did Miss X return to the front of the house and the pristine world of conventional order and appearance and not be moved to reach out for help? Why did she not call the police or fire department? And how could the therapy partnership understand the deep sense of confusion about what was real and what was imagined? Here the thought emerged that Miss X was tragically determined to stay attached to the mother at all costs. Her acceptance of suffering was the sacrifice she made to protect against total abandonment and her assumption of all the guilt in the relationship was an example of the "moral defence" (Fairbairn, 1952, p. 65) that allowed her to maintain the delusion of the good parents while she suffered the sacrificial fate of the bad child.

The question of her ability to trust her perceptions opened up the disorienting effects of the trauma that she experienced as her mother's world continued to collapse. Shengold (1989) identifies the way trauma breaks down the ego, its structures, and functions so that the subject loses confidence in her ability to know, authentically and with a body-based conviction, what has happened to her. As she said to herself as a teen: "This isn't happening to me!" If she believed her perceptions, she would be forced to realise her despair, fury, and absolute aloneness; if she denied her experience, she created a delusional experience predicated upon the manic belief that she might always be able to remain at the front of the house. The metaphor of the house revealed a radical state of splitting where she felt herself to be two different people and suggested a dissociative element in her defensive system.

Over the period of the next year the treatment examined the price Miss X paid in identifying with the perfect "front" of her mother and family's world and provided the means for considering the corruption and decay at the "back" of the house. As she discussed this dimension, she began to experience a depressed hopelessness that terrified her. She was able to acknowledge a cluster of suicidal ideas that she had held out of the treatment but said she was too mortified to explore them as they indicated she was more troubled than she could bear to consider. Though she consciously professed hatred towards her mother ("I don't care if she lives"), at an unconscious level she remained identified with her and in this way the love that she felt towards her "escaped extinction" (Freud, 1917e, p. 247).

The oscillating process between discovery and denial of the actual nature of her world, the two different registers of "front and back", drove Miss X into depressive experiences that began to show up as the psychosomatic conditions (beta states) of bowel problems and migraine headaches. The process of mourning could only be endured for brief moments as she struggled with a deep sense of abandonment that began to reveal how the battle between love and hate raged within her. If she began to experience the absence of her mother at the core of her psyche, she unleashed violent almost murderous attacks against herself as a sacrificial scapegoat and in this way used regressive suffering as part of her "private religion" (Freud, 1907b) to magically reconstitute the ideal object-mother. The sanctification of violence was revealed as her means to maintain control of the therapy relationship and she became able to consider how she maintained her fierce dependency on her mother at the cost of engaging in a genuine connection with the therapist. At the same time the struggle to give up the illusory object continued to occupy much of the therapeutic work.

The therapist's recognition of the grave balance between the life and death dynamics within Miss X, which had been hidden by the patient's long-term portrayal of her life at the "front" of the (therapy) house, and his own desire to stand at the "front" of his therapeutic identity, began to reveal the truly perilous position of the patient and the danger of his therapeutic ambitions. Feelings of sadness and humility at the poignancy of the situation, both within the patient and between the therapeutic partners, helped to reduce his countertransference frustrations and the pressure towards interpretation, and empowered the search for intuitive links comprised of empathy, reflection, and containment. The problems of resistance and impasse became more penetrable and the difference between mourning and melancholy (depression) could be seen and experienced in starker contrast.

On symbolising the unsymbolised

In *Learning from Experience* (1962) and subsequent works (1963, 1965, 1970), Bion describes his way of working towards the creation of mind, fostering an individual's capacities for thinking his or her own thoughts. In one particularly complex yet short paper, "Notes on memory and desire", Bion (1967) describes his clinical approach to the task of developing a capacity to think. Enigmatic and complex, as always, Bion shows us his thinking in such a way as to put the reader into a state of unknowing, having to suspend memory and desire in an attempt to grasp his ideas. As Bion describes his consistent attention towards the evolving, not yet-known of the session, the reader begins to apprehend Bion's tremendous faith in the creative process of psychoanalysis.

Memory, as Bion defines it, refers to the past, not a record of an experience as it happened but a record of the experience put through the condensing pressure cooker of unconscious phantasies, wishes, limited cognitive capacities, and homeostatic tendencies. Bear in mind that reflections of things the patient has talked about in the past are necessary. In my view, Bion is not urging us to "forget" what the patient has talked about in past sessions. Instead he is moving us towards taking all we know of the patient so far and holding that knowledge as provisional as we attend to what is emerging now, the previously unthought known (Bollas, 1987). Bion (1967) suggests we watch for the evolution, or absence of evolution, of a thought in each session, and this evolution must be observed as it is happening in the session.

Desire interferes with observations and judgements, forcing a selection or suppression of aspects of the experience according to the dictate of the desire. The therapist suspends judgements of the patient's behaviours about what the patient should do, or is not doing, working towards the fundamental experience of being, the being of experience and the experience of being oneself. Caution, as Bion (1967) states, must be applied to "[d]esires for results, 'cure' or even understanding must not be allowed to proliferate" (p. 18). Doing so allows the depth perception of experiences and thoughts, evolving from embryo to foetus, awash in the amniotic fluid of the unconscious, stirring but not yet emerging.

Signs of therapeutic desire, such as ambition, irritation, or comments by the therapist aimed to show sustained interest and even understanding, signal an attention directed towards what is expected or should be happening in the session. Instead, Bion urges our attention and curiosity towards unexpected evolutions and discoveries. Like Sancho Panza, we follow our Don Quixote patient, remaining loyal to the patient's view of the world and steadfast in our own minds as to the psychotherapeutic process.

In short, memory refers to what was supposed to have happened, and desire refers to what is supposed to happen in the future. Bion (1967) writes: "Psychoanalytic 'observation' is concerned neither with what has happened nor with what is going to happen but with what is happening" (p. 17). And he goes on to say: "What is 'known' about the patient is of no further consequence: it is either false or irrelevant. If it is 'known' by the patient and analyst, it is obsolete … The only point of importance in any session is the unknown. Nothing must be allowed to distract from intuiting that" (pp. 17–18).

This engagement calls for a quality of authenticity in the therapist, challenging the genuine contact of the therapist with herself in order to receive the signals from the patient. This is extremely challenging, especially when the patient is fearful, demanding, angry with the treatment, or disappointed that his hopes have not been met by the therapy. Pressures to "do" something abound, and we feel a pull to join the patient's defences rather than accept them as communications of a deep and painful trauma. Unbearable feelings in the therapist block receptivity to unbearable feelings in the patient.

Engaging with the patient in this way requires an interactive process, a "contemplative act" as Symington (2007b, p. 1421) describes it, taking place in the therapist in response to the patient. Inherent in this contemplation is recognition of the other as different, inexplicable, and autonomous. Often the therapist must wait for the emerging experience of the session without knowing, while tolerating doubts and fears. This kind of waiting can seem passive but actually takes tremendous effort: pausing without losing place, keeping one's thoughts in mind, not pushing, or expecting, and continuing to look into the dark, unsure of what might be there, a wild animal, a monster, or a goddess. Containment of the not-yet-known requires an active waiting, a waiting adjusted to the potential of this unknown. It is as if we prepare the soil for something to grow but we do not know what will germinate or if the seed will fail to take root.

Considering patients such as Miss X (see earlier), whose unbearable feelings remain bound up with the crying infant abandoned in the collapsed house while she, a potential maternal container for her infant self, turns away from claiming her maternal capacities and responsibilities. Instead, irritated that the neighbour, standing perhaps for the therapist, does not offer to help her enter the house, or protect her from the risk of collapse, she turns away, disavowing the internal reality she has discovered. The dream indicates the presence of a set of "perverse links" (Steiner, 1993, p. 12), perceiving the dreadful crisis occurring within her, and disavowing it at the same time, as if she can do so with impunity. Turning away from the crying infant, she also turns away from persecutory fears of unconscious guilt for having caused the neglect and subsequent abandonment of her infant. Her internal act of disavowal stops time, stops development and progress within the therapy. We imagine this internal reality extends through the transference to an irritation with the therapy and the potential to use the therapist to help her enter her collapsed and decrepit self, to seek the crying infant within her. Her decision to walk away indicates the tremendous pain and suffering she would endure should she decide to turn towards her suffering infant. At the same time, she walks away from the responsibility for developing herself and the possibility of delivering her baby-self into life through the creative and generative contact with the therapist. The therapist is called upon to sit with a patient whose abandoned baby faces possible death, an impending sacrifice of the infant self. Moving towards and containing extreme levels of helplessness and violence such as Miss X presents strains the limits of containment. And yet, with sustained attention to the helpless infant crying in the collapsed house, the therapist resonates with the terrible bind of the infant Miss X: unable to survive without a mother, and unequipped to be a mother to herself. Is it possible to give birth to these painful experiences through the generating warmth of the therapy relationship? How does the therapist survive the maternal containment of dead or dying internal objects without submerging into a powerful desire to rescue the dying infant?

Here the therapist might want to cajole, pressure, or reassure Miss X of her goodness. Or, alternatively, attribute the failure of progress in the therapy to the patient's refusal. Both responses would be deflections from containing Miss X's painful vulnerabilities and despair with her disowned infant-self and her wish to see only the front of the house, sparing her the work of mourning the loss of the mother and her consequent loss of self.

According to Bion (1962), as we understand, the communication and mutual experiencing between Miss X and the therapist of Miss X's suffering, potentially transforms Miss X's regressive suffering into a finite set of elements, acquiring personal meaning and significance, bound in time and space, expanding the thinking capacities of therapist and patient alike. The success of this process does not guarantee the achievement of progressive suffering, leading towards life and the acceptance of herself. With any patient, therapists face the limitations of ability and of the psychotherapy process: the potential for new internal objects to be born stands next to the possibility that a death will occur, a final death of a dying internal object, triggering a deep and painful mourning process, or a state of prolonged melancholia, a frozen mourning, and an addiction to near death, as Paul Koehler describes in Chapter Three, will continue unabated.

Bion (1967) urges us to attend to "the emotional experience" (p. 19) of the session, meaning experiences beyond the scope of the senses, such as sight, smell, hearing, taste, touch, attempting instead to register the raw experiences of anxiety, dread, depression, or joy and what it is like to be in these experiences. Working in this way we invite an encounter of what is happening in the moment, each moment new and not yet thought about. Bion suggests that the tolerance of empty space contains within it the creative, unrecognisable seed of the process of a thought coming into awareness. The spawning of unconscious thoughts, similar to the gestation of a baby in the dark, smooth world of the womb, brings Winnicott's (1967) theory of potential space to mind; an empty space allows for the birth of something new if the potential space can be tolerated without dread and persecution.

Symington (2007b) reminds us "that a mind has to be created" (p. 1410), and this creation takes place "through reflective communication with another" (p. 1410). The potential for psychic change expands through the reciprocal interactive aliveness between two people. An alive connection transmits desire to know and to be known in the present moment as it is happening in the session. Words, interpretations, and theories provide the conduit for the experience of getting to know. Psychoanalytic theories inform our thinking, preparing the backdrop to our work, and the most alive moments theory is reinvented now in a new form for this particular person in this specific time and place (Ogden, 2018).

Crying infant/hostile object

In her classic paper, "Addiction to near-death" (1982), Betty Joseph describes a particular category of highly resistant patients whose self-destructiveness can also be considered to be a sacrifice of a part of the self in lieu of the suffering of a proper parricide. As she describes, although many of these patients have not had, overtly, especially traumatic histories, their early experiences with their primary objects did not sufficiently prepare or fortify them to be able to bear the pain, ambivalence, and guilt that would inevitably begin to arise as they reached the threshold of the depressive position. That unmanageable pain would instead be experienced as inner torment. As Fairbairn (1943) has described, the indifference, the scornfulness, the rejection, the abandonment, or the abuse they suffered from their primary objects would, in an attempt to manage those experiences, be internalised and established as features of their internal world.

> I get the impression from the difficulty these patients experience in waiting and being aware of gaps and aware of even the simplest type of guilt that such potentially depressive experiences have been felt by them as terrible pain that goes over into torment, and that they have tried to obviate this by taking over the torment, the inflicting of mental pain on to themselves and building it into a world of perverse excitement, and this necessarily militates against any real progress towards the depressive position.
>
> It is very hard for our patients to find it possible to abandon such terrible delights for the uncertain pleasures of real relationships. (Joseph, 1982, pp. 454–455)

As Joseph describes, then, a part of the self, that part of the self still partially identified with its infantile omnipotence, is pitted against and chooses to sacrifice the parts of the self that might otherwise wish to grow, develop, and elaborate a particular and "novel" life. Moreover, the self is "enthralled" and held captive by the "terrible delights" to be experienced in continuous self-destructiveness.

In her paper, Joseph describes how this taking over of the torment becomes deployed in the transference. The healthy, libidinal, and, we might say, the potential parts of the self that might want to grow, develop, and separate are projected into the therapist, there to be forsaken, undermined, attacked, and scorned by the aggrieved and omnipotent parts of the self still sheltering inside the patient.

Here the need for containment that is strong and rigorous as well as generous and imaginative becomes essential. Joseph describes the necessity of distinguishing between the containment of the often acute feelings of despair and hopelessness, and the recognition of the masochistic and even triumphant use and exploitation of such feelings. When that recognition can be made, we will be better able to find a position where we are capable of recognising what might be possible in the therapy—and in the patient's life—without either being taken over by his despair in a way that substantiates his hopelessness or identifying with his inner tormentor and becoming critical or harsh.

As the therapist gradually becomes aware and cognisant of these dynamics, it can often eventuate in, among many other things, a feeling of dread in the countertransference. This dread is often a sign that the therapist is being recruited to receive the sacrifice of the potentially vital and hopeful parts of the patient that have been projected into the therapist. If the therapist can contain—and further symbolise—the feeling of dread, it often can lead to further and deeper understanding of the patient's internal world. In a concordant identification (Racker, 1968) it can evoke a more palpable sense of the patient's despair about ever making generative contact with another object. And, on the other hand, apprehending how our dread can prompt a desire to turn away from or otherwise scorn the patient can prompt us to recognise a complementary identification with such an object in the patient's internal world.

One of our supervisees brought a recently started case for supervision. The patient was a sixty-year-old woman who for many years previously had been seen by a therapist before that therapist retired. The patient lived with her husband and had a daughter who was living on her own. The patient's complaints were of chronic depression and anxiety. She hadn't worked for several years, was obese, and spent much of her time in bed. In her current therapy, according to her therapist, she often cried like a child and otherwise filled her sessions with detailed sarcastic complaints about the many people—mother, father, husband, and daughter—who she felt had failed her. Whenever her therapist attempted, even obliquely, to suggest that the patient bear some responsibility for her plight and might be able to do something herself to improve it, she was met with a scornful rebuke and a refusal even to consider such a possibility.

Her therapist, experiencing something of a double consciousness, both dreaded her sessions with her, while also feeling desperate to help her:

> I find I think about her all the time, far more than I want to. I try hard to empathise with her, but whenever I seem, even slightly, to make emotional contact with her, she finds a way to throw it back in my face. I think to myself, with her, no good deed goes unpunished.

Discussing the case in supervision, the therapist began to experience something of the containment that she herself was trying, but not quite succeeding, to provide for her patient. She was able to find more space to consider—and in a certain way more fully to suffer and therefore to symbolise—the dread, the hatred, and, finally, the helpless despair that her patient evoked in her. The supervisor and the therapist then began to apprehend that the therapist was both encountering, and being prompted to identify with, a particular object in the patient's internal world. Although the contours and characteristics of that object were only now beginning to come into focus, they could begin to imagine an object that was at best indifferent to or otherwise hostile to the patient's life and liveliness. They could then begin to recognise in the patient's persistent crying in the sessions the remnants of her infant self, alone and despairing in her crib, desperately trying to make contact with a mother hostilely unable to comfort or contain her.

As the therapist recognised and disengaged from the attempted sacrifice both of her own wellbeing and her capacity to think symbolically, the patient began more properly to suffer her own despair. The therapist found herself less preoccupied with her patient when she was not in a session with her. And she noticed that her patient's tears, although still prodigious, began to reflect less a sense of demand and accusation and more a quality suggesting true mourning.

The sacrifice that saves

The *Encyclopædia Britannica* defines sacrifice as "a celebration of life" and states that through it the victim (i.e., the scapegoat) attains a "sacred potency that establishes a bond between the sacrificer and the sacred power." In the private religion of the traumatised patient, the sacrifice of parts of self—namely, those parts that are subject to judgement, hatred, evacuation, and projection—is repeated compulsively not only in order to eliminate shame and guilt, but also to *save and consecrate*, through gaining access to the god-object, the life that the subject feels he has left, after the psychic subtractions have been effectuated by past trauma. This double-sided purpose of the patient's sacrifice highlights the dual nature of his desire. These patients want, at the same time, to annihilate within themselves all traces of their trauma *and* to carve out, "within the square inch of [their] own mind" (Bodhidharma, sixth century CE—see Broughton, 1999, p. 12), a place of safety, where the nucleus of self can hide, as in a bomb shelter, until the war beyond it is over and it can emerge to find a way to regain its liveliness.

We recognise that such divisions in the patient's self and desire must remain in the therapist's awareness throughout the course of treatment. It is too common for therapists to focus only on one side or the other of the patient's divided self, ignoring either the desire to sacrifice or the desire to live that undergird the patient's dilemma. For the therapist, however, to be caught in limiting interpretations of only one side of the patient's dilemma is to ask of the patient that they abandon their defences without addressing what will happen with their *other* desire. In such a case, the patient will realise that the treatment does not present them with a better solution to their dilemma than their own. As Steiner (2019) and Sodré (2015) have noted, the patient's "method of cure" is often in profound conflict with the therapist's, and the therapist's cure is inevitably seen by the patient "as an interference" with his own (Steiner, 2019, p. 17).

The cure the therapist offers to the traumatised patient can be stated simply, though in reality its basic steps are terrifying to the patient. They include: drawing the patient towards mourning the reality of their trauma, rather than retreating from it into an embrace with a comforting but ultimately stultifying ideal mother or god-object; diverting the patient's object-cathexis away from the ideal mother and towards real objects in an interpersonal world; and liberating the patient from an internal regimen (in which the patient is trapped between a harsh and accusatory superego and the god-object) that convinces the patient of the necessity of sacrifice as a means of both healing the damaged object and of avoiding guilt and shame for having been the source of that damage. Through consistent interpretations, stable and unflinching neutrality, and a willingness to analyse the nuances of countertransference thoughts, images, and emotions, the therapist slowly helps the patient towards these goals, albeit according to a meandering path that is unique to each patient.

Analysis of countertransference, in particular, is of primary importance when working with these patients, since it is often through the therapist's awareness of the interpersonal sources of countertransferential reactions that insight can be gained into the lost or dissociated aspects of the patient's experience. An example of the usefulness of such analyses comes from a fifty-three-year-old patient who entered therapy because she'd had no romantic relationships for twenty-five years and felt stuck in a job she didn't like. In one session, the patient complained that all she did was work, go home, go to sleep, and get up to start over again the next day. "I don't even have any hobbies," the patient said. "I don't know how to play. I never played as a child. I was always too anxious. I couldn't let myself go that much. And I still don't know how to play. I need to figure out how. Do you have any suggestions?"

The therapist's first impression, upon hearing the patient's question, was that she wasn't serious. Her wooden, impassive, and deliberate tone, he thought, could not be a tone that accompanied a serious desire to learn to play. Besides, he wondered, how does one person even teach another to play? It seemed like an impossible task. Playing, he thought, can't be accomplished through willful deliberateness. It is not something that one *does*. It is something that one *is*. "But how do I convey this to a patient who has never experienced it?" he asked himself, and as he did so he realised he was feeling yet another emotion, one that referred more viscerally to the "present moment" (Stern, 2004) he was sharing with his patient: he was feeling stymied and constrained, as though he had lost access to his own creativity—his own capacity to play—by taking the patient's request too literally. The correspondence between the patient's initial complaint of her inability to play and the state of non-creativity the therapist now found himself in was quite striking, and the therapist now wondered what had been communicated to him from the patient that had so effectively shut down the liveliness of his mind.

It was at this point that a purely spontaneous image appeared to the therapist. It was of two full plates, brimming with food but untouched, sitting on the side table next to where the patient was sitting. Accompanying the image was a vague feeling/thought, along the lines of "Huh? Two plates of food and neither of us get to eat?" With this image in mind, the therapist now felt he had a better understanding of the unconscious interplay between himself and the patient. To be sure, the patient's conscious request for suggestions about how to play told the therapist she experienced herself as unskilled and unpractised at playing, and as wanting to learn. Unconsciously, however, she conveyed to him—through the medium of projective identification and the therapist's unconscious resonance with her projected material—that (1) she was frightened of play in general, (2) she was unwilling to play in the moment, and (3) she had projected her desire to play into the therapist in order to collapse the potential for playing through her overly pragmatic request and her detached and apathetic tone. This latter point bears elaboration. The therapist learned, particularly through the image of two plates of food that neither could eat, that the patient *authentically* wanted to play and to live her life spontaneously, but that she was so frightened of the consequences of such spontaneity that she had developed automatic mechanisms within her mind to suppress her desires—to the point that if she experienced them at all, she only felt them to be empty simulacra that had no capacity for generating lively experience.

The therapist was now able to speak to the patient. He told her that their interaction had revealed something important about her relationship with her own mind. When she asked him for suggestions about learning to play, he said, she had been feeling the familiar fear of letting her mind go and making the spontaneous products of her mind visible. In response to this fear, she had attempted to assign the task of learning to play to the therapist, and she had done it in such a restrained way that the possibility of play, either in her, in the therapist, or between the two, was automatically smothered. "If I were to engage with you in those terms," the therapist said, "if I were to give you suggestions, like a teacher, for learning to play, I would be taking my place in that same detached, deliberate but ultimately stultifying space. There might be something helpful about it to you," he added,

> but only to a certain extent. More importantly, it would mean that I had joined you in fear, and the two of us would have then been complicit in suppressing the potential spontaneity of the moment. And that would have meant we had left behind the part of you that longs to play and that is grieving the fact that you haven't played as much as you've wanted in your life.

The patient's reaction to this interpretation was not immediate. It was only over the course of multiple subsequent sessions that the full meaning of the dilemma she faced became fully fleshed out. But it is important to note that it was the therapist's *refusal* to engage in a countertransference enactment—one that would have collapsed his mind and narrowed his understanding of his patient—that allowed him to begin to comprehend the patient's need to sacrifice herself in order to remain safe in her internal environment—despite the fact that she also longed to be free of the necessity of such sacrifice. By paying attention to the subtle, unconscious communications he had received from his patient, the therapist was able to begin the slow process of symbolising the unsymbolised, of containing that which had been split off and denied, and of thereby helping the patient engage in the essential psychic work of mourning the legacy of past traumas.

References

Asch, S. S. (1976). Varieties of negative therapeutic reactions and problems of technique. *Journal of the American Psychoanalytic Association, 24*: 383–407.

Auster, P. (1994). *Mr. Vertigo*. New York: Penguin.

Baranger, W. (1974). A discussion of the paper by Helena Besserman Vianna on "A Peculiar Form of Resistance to Psycho-Analytical Treatment". *International Journal of Psycho-Analysis, 55*: 445–447.

Bergmann, M. (1992). *In the Shadow of Moloch: The Sacrifice of Children and Its Impact on Western Religions*. New York: Columbia University Press.

Bergstein, A. (2019). *Bion and Meltzer's Expeditions into Unmapped Mental Life*. London: Routledge.

Berlioz, H. (1856). Letter, November 1856. In P. Citron (Ed.), *Correspondance Générale*. Paris, Flammarion, 1989. Translation found in Davies, P. (1996). *About Time: Einstein's Unfinished Revolution*. New York: Simon & Schuster, p. 214.

Bion, W. R. (1948). *Experiences in Groups*. London: Tavistock, 1961.

Bion, W. R. (1957). On arrogance. In: *Second Thoughts: Selected Papers on Psychoanalysis*. London: Karnac, 2007.

Bion, W. R. (1962). *Learning from Experience*. New York: Jason Aronson

Bion, W. R. (1963). *Elements of Psycho-Analysis*. In *Seven Servants*. New York: Jason Aronson, 1977.

Bion, W. R. (1965). *Transformations*. In *Seven Servants*. New York: Jason Aronson, 1977.

Bion, W. R. (1967). Notes on memory and desire. In E. Spillius (Ed.), *Melanie Klein Today: Developments in Theory and Practice; Volume 2: Mainly Practice* (pp. 17–21). London: Routledge, 1988.

Bion, W. R. (1970). *Attention and Interpretation*. In *Seven Servants*. New York: Jason Aronson, 1977.

Bion, W. R. (1997). *Taming Wild Thoughts*. F. Bion (Ed.). London: Karnac.

Bollas, C. (1987). *The Shadow of the Object: Psychoanalysis of the Unthought Known*. New York: Columbia University Press.

Bollas, C. (1995). *Cracking Up—The Work of Unconscious Experience*. London: Routledge.

Bowlby, J. (1958). The nature of the child's tie to his mother. *International Journal of Psycho-Analysis, 39*: 350–373.

Britton, R. S. (2003). *Sex, Death and the Super-ego*. London: Karnac.

Broughton, J. L. (1999). *The Bodhidharma Anthology: The Earliest Records of Zen*. Berkeley, CA: University of California Press.

Cervantes, M. (2005). *Don Quixote*. E. Grossman (Trans.). New York: Harper Collins.

Chasseguet-Smirgel, J. (1985a). *Creativity and Perversion*. London: Free Association Books.

Chasseguet-Smirgel, J. (1985b). *The Ego Ideal: A Psychoanalytic Essay on the Malady of the Ideal*. New York: Norton.

Chasseguet-Smirgel, J. (1986). *Sexuality and Mind: The Role of the Father and Mother in the Psyche*. New York: New York University Press.

Civitarese, G. (2008). *The Intimate Room: Theory and Technique of the Analytic Field*. London: Routledge.

Civitarese, G. (2013). *The Violence of Emotions: Bion and Post-Bionian Psychoanalysis*. London: Routledge.

Civitarese, G. (2016a). Masochism and its rhythm. *Journal of the American Psychoanalytic Association 64(5)*: 885–916.

Civitarese, G. (2016b). *Truth and the Unconscious in Psychoanalysis*. London: Routledge.

Civitarese, G. (2019). The concept of time in Bion's "A Theory of Thinking". *International Journal of Psychoanalysis, 100(2)*: 182–205.

Cohen, M. (1993). The negative therapeutic reaction, maternal transference, and obsessions. *American Journal of Psychoanalysis, 53*: 123–136.

Davoine, F. (2016). *Fighting Melancholia: Don Quixote's Teaching*. London: Karnac.

Davoine, F., & Gaudillière, J-M. (2004). *History Beyond Trauma: Whereof One Cannot Speak, Thereof One Cannot Stay Silent*. S. Fairfield (Trans.). New York: Other Press.

Fairbairn, W. R. D. (1943). The repression and return of bad objects (with special reference to the 'war neuroses'). In *Psychoanalytic Studies of the Personality* (pp. 59–81). London: Routledge, 1960.

Fairbairn, W. R. D. (1952). *Psychoanalytic Studies of the Personality*. London: Routledge.

Ferro, A. (2005). *Seeds of Illness, Seeds of Recovery: The Genesis of Suffering and the Role of Psychoanalysis*. New York: Brunner-Routledge.

Ferro, A. & Civitarese, G. (2015). *The Analytic Field and its Transformations*. London: Karnac.

Finell, J. W. (1987). A challenge to psychoanalysis: A review of the negative therapeutic reaction. *Psychoanalytic Review, 74(4)*: 487–515.

Fornari, F. (1975). *The Psychoanalysis of War*. Bloomington: Indiana University Press.

Freud, S. (1905d). *Three Essays on the Theory of Sexuality. S. E., 7*: 135–243. London: Hogarth.

Freud, S. (1907b). *Obsessive actions and religious practices. S. E., 9*: 117–127. London: Hogarth.

Freud, S. (1909c). *Family romances. S. E., 9*: 237–241. London: Hogarth.

Freud, S. (1910e). *The antithetical meaning of primal words. S. E., 11*: 155–161. London: Hogarth.

Freud, S. (1914c). *On narcissism: An introduction. S. E., 14*: 73–104. London: Hogarth.

Freud, S. (1915a). *The unconscious. S. E., 14*: 159–215. London: Hogarth.

Freud, S. (1917e). *Mourning and melancholia. S. E., 14*: 243–258. London: Hogarth.

Freud, S. (1920g). *Beyond the Pleasure Principle. S. E., 18*: 1–64. London: Hogarth.

Freud, S. (1923b). *The Ego and the Id. S. E., 19*: 12–66. London: Hogarth.

Freud, S. (1924d). *The dissolution of the Oedipus complex. S. E., 19*: 173–179. London: Hogarth.

Freud, S. (1927e). *Fetishism. S. E., 21*: 149–157. London: Hogarth.

Freud, S. (1930a). *Civilization and its Discontents. S. E., 21*: 57–146. London: Hogarth.

Freud, S. (1937c). *Analysis terminable and interminable. S. E., 209–253*. London: Hogarth.

Gabbard, G. O. (1996). *Love and Hate in the Analytic Setting*. Northvale, NJ: Jason Aronson.

Ganssle, G. E. (2017). God and time. In J. Fieser & B. Dowden (Eds.), *Internet Encyclopedia of Philosophy: A Peer-Reviewed Academic Resource* (Online journal) at www.iep.utm.edu/god-time/#SH1a

Garland, C. (1998). Thinking about trauma. In C. Garland (Ed.), *Understanding Trauma* (pp. 9–31). London: Routledge.

Girard, R. (1977). *Violence and the Sacred*. P. Gregory (Trans.). Baltimore, MD: Johns Hopkins University Press.

Girard, R. (1986). *The Scapegoat*. Baltimore, MD: Johns Hopkins University Press.

Glenn, J. (1984). A note on loss, pain and masochism in children. *Journal of the American Psychoanalytic Association, 32*: 63–73.

Graves, R. (1955). *The Greek Myths, Vol. 2*. Baltimore: Penguin.

Green, A. (1975). The analyst, symbolisation and absence in the analytic setting (On changes in analytic practice and analytic experience)—in memory of D. W. Winnicott. *International Journal of Psycho-Analysis, 56*: 1–22.

Green, A. (1986). The dead mother. In *On Private Madness* (pp. 142–173). London: Hogarth (reprinted London: Karnac, 1997).

Green, A. (2002). A dual conception of narcissism: Positive and negative organisations. *Psychoanalytic Quarterly, 71(4)*: 631–649.

Greene, W. C. (1944). *Moira: Fate, Good, & Evil* in *Greek Thought*. New York: Harper Torchbooks, 1963.

Grotstein, J. (1979). Demoniacal possession, splitting and the torment of joy: A psychoanalytic inquiry into the negative therapeutic reaction. *Contemporary Psychoanalysis, 15*: 407–445.

Grotstein, J. S. (1997). Why Oedipus and not Christ?: A psychoanalytic inquiry into innocence, human sacrifice, and the sacred—Part II: The numinous and spiritual dimension as a metapsychological perspective. *American Journal of Psychoanalysis, 57(4)*: 317–335.

Grotstein, J. (2000). Why Oedipus and not Christ, Part 1. In *Who is the Dreamer Who Dreams the Dream?* (pp. 219–253). Hillsdale, NJ: The Analytic Press.

Grotstein, J. S. (2007). *A Beam of Intense Darkness: Wilfred Bion's Legacy to Psychoanalysis*. London: Karnac.

Grotstein, J. S. (2009). *"... But at the Same Time and on Another Level ...": Psychoanalytic Theory and Technique in the Kleinian/Bionian Mode.* (Vol. 1) London: Karnac.

Grunberger, B. (1989). *New Essays on Narcissism.* D. Macey (Ed. & Trans.). London: Free Association Books.

Hartocollis, P. (1983). *Time and Timelessness: The Varieties of Temporal Experience.* New York: International Universities Press.

Heidegger, M. (1927/1962). *Being and Time.* J. Macquarrie & E. Robinson (Trans.). New York: Harper & Row.

Homer (1998). *The Iliad.* R. Fables (Trans.). London: Penguin Books.

Jaffe, D. S. (1988). Psychoanalytic principles and principle deviations. *Annual of Psychoanalysis, 16*: 55–79.

Jarrell, R. (1962). On preparing to read Kipling. In E. Gilbert (Ed.), *Kipling and the Critics* (pp. 133–149). New York: New York University Press, 1965.

Joseph, B. (1982). Addiction to near-death. *International Journal of Psycho-Analysis, 63*: 449–456.

Kafka, F. (1922). A hunger artist. In W. Muir & E. Muir (Trans.), *Franz Kafka: The Penal Colony: Shorts and Short Pieces* (pp. 243–256). New York: Schocken Books, 1948.

Kant, E. (1992). *Cambridge Companion to Kant.* P. Guyer (Ed.). Cambridge: Cambridge University Press.

Kernberg, O. (1995). *Love Relations: Normality and Pathology*. New Haven, CT: Yale University Press.

Klein, M. (1928). Early stages of the Oedipus complex. In Money-Kyrle, R. (Ed.), *The Writings of Melanie Klein, Vol. I: Love, Guilt and Reparation and Other Works 1921–1945* (pp. 186–198). New York: Free Press, 1975.

Klein, M. (1935). A contribution to the psychogenesis of manic-depressive states. In *The Writings of Melanie Klein, Vol 1, Love, Guilt and Reparation and Other Works 1921–1945* (pp. 262–289). New York: Delacorte Press.

Klein, M. (1945). The Oedipus complex in light of early anxieties. In Money-Kyrle, R. (Ed.), *The Writings of Melanie Klein, Vol. I: Love, Guilt and Reparation and Other Works 1921–1945* (pp. 370–419). New York: Free Press, 1975.

Klein, M. (1946). Notes on some schizoid mechanisms. In *The Writings of Melanie Klein, Vol 3., Envy and Gratitude and Other Works 1946–1963* (pp. 1–24). New York: Delacorte Press.

Klein, M. (1948). On the theory of anxiety and guilt. In Money-Kyrle, R. (Ed.), *The Writings of Melanie Klein, Vol. III: Envy and Gratitude and Other Works 1946–1963* (pp. 25–42). New York: The Free Press, 1975.

Klein, M. (1952). The mutual influences in the development of ego and id. In Money-Kyrle, R. (Ed.), *The Writings of Melanie Klein, Vol. III: Envy and Gratitude and Other Works 1946–1963* (pp. 57–60). New York: The Free Press, 1975.

Klein, M. (1957). Envy and gratitude. In Money-Kyrle, R. (Ed.), *The Writings of Melanie Klein, Vol. III: Envy and Gratitude and Other Works 1946–1963* (pp. 176–235). New York: The Free Press, 1975.

Klein, M. (1963a). On the sense of loneliness. In Money-Kyrle, R. (Ed.), *The Writings of Melanie Klein, Vol. III: Envy and Gratitude and Other Works 1946–1963* (pp. 300–313). New York: The Free Press, 1975.

Klein, M. (1963b). Some reflections on 'The Oresteia.' In Money-Kyrle, R. (Ed.), *The Writings of Melanie Klein, Vol. III: Envy and Gratitude and Other Works 1946–1963* (pp. 275–299). New York: The Free Press, 1975.

Kohon, G. (1999). Dreams, acting out and symbolic impoverishment. In *No Lost Certainties to Be Recovered* (pp. 73–86). London: Karnac.

Kohut, H. (1972). Thoughts on narcissism and narcissistic rage. *Psychoanalytic Study of the Child, 27*: 360–400.

Lacan, J. (1977). *Écrits: A Selection*. A. Sheridan (Trans.). London: Tavistock.

Loewald, H. W. (1972). Freud's conception of the negative therapeutic reaction, with comments on instinct theory. *Journal of the American Psychoanalytic Association, 20*: 235–245.

Loewald, H. (1979). The waning of the Oedipus complex. In *Papers on Psychoanalysis* (384–404). New Haven, CT: Yale University Press, 1980.

Lombardi, R. (2016). *Formless Infinity: Clinical Explorations of Matte Blanco and Bion*. K. Christenfeld, G. Atkinson, A. Sabbadini, & P. Slotkin (Trans.). London: Routledge.

Lombardi, R. (2017). The body in the analytic session: focusing on the body-mind link. In *Body-Mind Dissociation in Psychoanalysis* (pp. 92–109). London: Routledge.

McDougall, J. (1980). *Plea for a Measure of Abnormality*. New York: International Universities Press.

McDougall, J. (1982). The narcissistic economy and its relation to primitive sexuality. *Contemporary Psychoanalysis, 18*: 373–396.

McDougall, J. (1995). *The Many Faces of Eros: A Psychoanalytic Exploration of Human Sexuality*. New York: Norton.

Merriam Webster online dictionary at www.merriam-webster.com/

Money-Kyrle, R. (1971). The aim of psycho-analysis. *International Journal of Psycho-Analysis, 52*: 103–106. Reprinted in *The Collected Papers of Roger Money-Kyrle* (pp. 416–433). Strath Tay: Clunie Press, 1978.

Nagy, G. (1979). *The Best of the Achaeans*. Baltimore, MD: John Hopkins University Press.

Neumann, E. (1954). *The Origins and History of Consciousness*. New York: Princeton University Press, 1970.

Nietzsche, F. (1994). *On the Genealogy of Morality*. C. Diethe (Trans.). Cambridge: Cambridge University Press.

Novick, J., & Novick, K. K. (1991) Some comments on masochism and the delusion of omnipotence from a developmental perspective. *Journal of the American Psychoanalytic Association, 39*: 307–331.

Novick, J., & Novick, K. K. (1996). *Fearful Symmetry: The Development and Treatment of Sadomasochism*. Latham: Rowman & Littlefield.

Ogden, T. H. (1986). *The Matrix of the Mind*. New York: Jason Aronson.

Ogden, T. H. (2002). A new reading of the origins of object-relations theory. *International Journal of Psycho-Analysis, 83*: 767–782.

Ogden, T. H. (2005). *This Art of Psychoanalysis: Dreaming Undreamt Dreams and Interrupted Cries*. London: Routledge.

Ogden, T. H. (2009). *Rediscovering Psychoanalysis: Thinking, and Dreaming, Learning and Forgetting*. London: Routledge.

Ogden, T. H. (2016). Dark ironies of the "gift" of consciousness: Kafka's "A hunger artist". In *Reclaiming Unlived Life: Experiences in Psychoanalysis* (pp. 115–138). London: Routledge.

Ogden, T. H. (2018). How I talk with my patients. *The Psychoanalytic Quarterly, 87(3)*: 399–413.

Ogden, T. H. (2019). Ontological psychoanalysis or "what do you want to be when you grow up?" *Psychoanalytic Quarterly, 88(4)*: 661–684.

Online Etymological Dictionary at www.etymonline.com/

Otto, R. (1923). *The Idea of the Holy*. J. W. Harvey (Trans.). London: Oxford University Press.

Pontalis, J. B. (1980). The negative therapeutic reaction: An attempt at definition. *Bulletin of the European Psychoanalytical Federation, 15*, 619–641.

Pontalis, J. B. (2014). No, twice no: An attempt to define and dismantle the 'negative therapeutic reaction'. *International Journal of Psycho-Analysis, 95(3)*: 533–551.

Poulton, J. L. (2013). *Object Relations and Relationality in Couple Therapy: Exploring the Middle Ground*. Lanham, MD: Jason Aronson.

Racker, H. (1968). *Transference and Countertransference*. New York: International Universities Press.

Riviere, J. (1936). A contribution to the analysis of the negative therapeutic reaction. *International Journal of Psycho-Analysis, 17*: 304–320. Reprinted in A. Hughes (Ed.) *The Inner World and Joan Riviere: Collected Papers*. London: Karnac, 1991.

Rosenfeld, H. (1971). A clinical approach to the psychoanalytic theory of the life and death instincts: An investigation into the aggressive aspects of narcissism. *International Journal of Psycho-Analysis, 52*: 169–178.

Rosenfeld, H. (1975). Negative therapeutic reaction. In P. L. Giovacchini (Ed.), *Tactics and Techniques in Psychoanalytic Therapy (Vol. 2)* (pp. 217–228). New York: Jason Aronson.

Sandler, J. (1976a). Countertransference and role responsiveness. *International Review of Psycho-Analysis, 3*: 43–47.

Sandler, J., Dare, C., & Holder, A. (1973/1992). *The Patient and the Analyst: The Basis of the Psychoanalytic Process (2nd Edition)*. London: Karnac.

Scharff, J. S. (1992). *Projective and Introjective Identification and the Use of the Therapist's Self*. Northvale, NJ: Jason Aronson.

Schmithüsen, G. (2013). "Time that no one can count, always begins anew": Thoughts concerning the function and meaning of the so-called negative therapeutic reaction from the perspective of time standing still. In L. Wurmser & H. Jarass (Eds.), *Nothing Good is Allowed to Stand: An Integrative View of the Negative Therapeutic Reaction* (pp. 67–96). London: Routledge.

Segal, H. (1957). 'Notes on symbol formation', *International Journal of Psycho-Analysis, 38*: 391–7.

Segal, H. (1987). Silence is the real crime. *International Review of Psycho-Analysis, 14*: 3–12.

Segal, H. (1992). Acting on phantasy and acting on desire. In *Yesterday, Today and Tomorrow* (pp. 96–113). London: Routledge, 2007.

Shakespeare, W. (1605). *The Tragedy of Macbeth*. Baltimore, MD: Penguin, 1956.

Shay, J. (1994). *Achilles in Vietnam*. New York: Scribner.

Shengold, L. (1989). *Soul Murder: The Effects of Childhood Abuse and Deprivation*. New Haven, CT: Yale University Press.

Shengold, L. (1995). *Delusions of Everyday Life*. New Haven, CT: Yale University Press.

Sodré, I. (2015). 'For ever wilt thou love, and she be fair!': On Quixotism and the golden age of pre-genital sexuality. In P. Roth (Ed.) *Imaginary Existences: A Psychoanalytic Exploration of Phantasy, Fiction, Dreams and Daydreams* (pp. 105–120). London: Routledge.

Spitz, R. A. (1965). *The First Year of Life*. New York: International Universities Press.

Steiner, J. (1993). *Psychic Retreats: Pathological Organisations in Psychotic, Neurotic and Borderline Patients*. London: Routledge.

Steiner, J. (2005). The conflict between mourning and melancholia. *Psychoanalytic Quarterly, 74(1)*: 83–104.

Steiner, J. (2011). *Seeing and Being Seen: Emerging from a Psychic Retreat*. London: Routledge.

Steiner, J. (2019). Learning from Don Quixote. Paper delivered at West Lodge Conference, London, 29–31 March 2019.

Stern, D. N. (2004). *The Present Moment in Psychotherapy and Everyday Life*. New York: Norton.

Stoller, R. J. (1975). *Perversion: The Erotic Form of Hatred*. London: Karnac,1986.

Symington, N. (1983). The analyst's act of freedom as agent of therapeutic change. *International Review of Psycho-Analysis, 10*: 283–291.

Symington, N. (2002). *A Pattern of Madness*. London: Karnac.

Symington, N. (2007a). *Becoming a Person Through Psychoanalysis*. London: Karnac.

Symington, N. (2007b). A technique for facilitating the creation of mind. *International Journal of Psycho-Analysis, 88(6)*: 1409–1422.

Symington, N. (2017). "Growth of the mind". February–April 2017. Lecture series by video link.

Tustin, F. (1972). *Autism and Childhood Psychosis*. London: Hogarth.

Valenstein, A. F. (1973). On attachment to painful feelings and the negative therapeutic reaction. *Psychoanalytic Study of the Child, 28*: 365–392. New Haven, CT: Yale University Press.

Von Leyden, W. (1964). Time, number, and eternity in Plato and Aristotle. *The Philosophical Quarterly, 14(54)*: 35–52.

Welles, J. K., and Wrye, H. K. (1991). The maternal erotic countertransference. *International Journal of Psycho-Analysis, 72*: 93–106

Winnicott, D. W. (1945). Primitive emotional development. In *Through Paediatrics to Psycho-Analysis* (pp. 145–156). New York: Basic Books, 1958.

Winnicott, D. W. (1951). Transitional objects and transitional phenomena: A study of the first not-me possession. In *Through Paediatrics to Psychoanalysis: Collected Papers* (pp. 229–242). London: Tavistock, 1958.

Winnicott, D. W. (1956). Primary maternal preoccupation. In *Through Paediatrics to Psycho-analysis* (pp. 300–305). London: The Hogarth Press and the Institute of Psycho-Analysis, 1975.

Winnicott, D. W. (1960). Ego distortion in terms of true and false self. In *The Maturational Processes and the Facilitating Environment: Studies in the Theory of Emotional Development* (pp. 140–157). Madison, CT: International Universities Press, 1965.

Winnicott, D. W. (1962). Ego integration in child development. In *The Maturational Processes and the Facilitating Environment: Studies in the Theory of Emotional Development* (pp. 56–63). Madison, CT: International Universities Press, 1965.

Winnicott, D. W. (1967). The location of cultural experience. *International Journal of Psycho-Analysis, 48*: 368–372.

Winnicott, D. W. (1971). *Playing and Reality*. London: Tavistock.

Winnicott, D. W. (1974). Fear of breakdown. *International Review of Psycho-Analysis, 1*: 103–107.

Wurmser, L. (2007). *Torment Me But Don't Abandon Me*. Northvale, NJ: Jason Aronson.

Wurmser, L. (2013). Negative therapeutic reaction and the compulsion to disappoint the other. In L. Wurmser & H. Jarass (Eds.), *Nothing Good Is Allowed to Stand: An Integrative View of the Negative Therapeutic Reaction* (pp. 27–56). London: Routledge.

Wurmser, L., & Jarass, H. (2013a). Introduction. In L. Wurmser & H. Jarass (Eds.), *Nothing Good is Allowed to Stand: An Integrative View of the Negative Therapeutic Reaction* (pp. 1–25). New York and London: Routledge.

Wurmser, L., & Jarass, H. (2013b). *Nothing Good is Allowed to Stand: An Integrative View of the Negative Therapeutic Reaction*. New York: Routledge.

Index